True Spoken English

Secrets to Speaking English

By Bill Grout

Published by New Sun Publications

Half Moon Bay, California

For Information contact:

True Spoken English

227 Granelli Ave, Half Moon Bay, Ca 94019.

Email: info@truespokenenglish.com

About True Spoken English

Welcome to True Spoken English.

These simple lessons will teach you secrets to speaking English. They will teach you common pronunciation changes that English speakers make. These changes are informal and rarely taught to a person learning English. But these changes are made by almost all English speakers.

By learning these changes, you'll understand English more easily, and your English will sound more like a native speaker.

You'll find these changes easy to learn and they will speed up your speaking and fluency.

You'll learn these changes by watching simple movies. As you watch the movies, you can listen to the lessons and practice speaking English. The lessons are easy, and you don't need to know a lot of English in order to take them.

True Spoken English provides 22 lessons and over 97 video exercises that present common pronunciation changes. These are everyday changes that English speakers make in conversation. And you need to know them to speak English well.

Learning the pronunciation changes will help you better understand informal English conversations, increase the fluency and speed of your speech, and help you sound more like a native speaker.

Instructions for Using True Spoken English Book and DVDs

This book and DVD set present the same video lessons available on at the website www.truespokenenglish.com. The True Spoken English book presents the text of the 22 lessons provided in the course.

The three DVDs present the 22 video lessons and all their exercises. These lessons can be played on a DVD player connected to a TV, or played in a DVD player connected to your computer. If your computer is capable of playing a DVD, it can play the True Spoken English DVD lessons.

Disc 1 contains lessons 1 through 8.
Disc 2 contains lessons 9 through 16.
Disc 3 contains lessons 17 through 22.

To use the True Spoken English book and DVDs together, insert a DVD in your DVD player, select the lesson you want to take on your TV or computer screen, and then turn to that lesson in the book to follow along with the text, if you choose. The video lessons include all explanations provided in the book, so you don't need to follow along in the book if you don't want to. But it's a good idea to follow along in the book to help you see and get used to any vocabulary that may be unfamiliar to you.

As you watch, be sure to practice saying the pronunciation changes out loud. Practicing out loud will enable to use the changes easily and casually in your English conversations later. You'll find that each lesson teaches and reviews the pronunciation changes in small steps. And by the end of the 22 lessons, you'll find that your informal conversation has changed a surprising amount, as you use the many full-speed changes that native English speakers naturally use.

Table of Contents

Lesson 1: Want to Wants to

Introduction

When I talk to others in friendly conversation, I often speed up my speech. I change words to make them faster to say.

For example, when I speak to other friends, I pronounce "want to" as "wanta." I say to friends, "I wanta see a movie." I say "I want to see a movie" in a formal conversation or when I want to be clear. But in casual conversation, I use "wanta"; I say, "I wanta" "I wanta see a movie." It's much faster and my English speaking friends all understand and make this change as they speak.

So, as a person learning English, you must know about this change if you want to clearly understand what is said to you. And you should use this change, too, to make your English sound more conversational, more like a native speaker.

There are many English changes like this. And in this course you'll hear and practice the most common ones. It'll help your understanding of casual English, and improve the sound and speed of your conversation.

Let's get started with a short first lesson.

Exercise 1 Present: Want to

Let's look closer at a common change, listen.

I wanta go fishing. I wanta go fishing.

The words "want to" can change to "wanta," the word "to" is pronounced "ta" and sounds the same as word "the." This "uh" sound is often used in the changes you'll learn here.

Listen

I wanta go surfing.
I wanta go surfing.

Read

I wanta go surfing.

Next, let's practice this change.

Exercise 2 Repeat (reading)

For practice, say these sentences slowly.

I wanta go surfing.

I wanta go fishing.

I wanta go jogging.

I wanta go biking.

I wanta go kayaking.

Repeat (reading)

Now say these sentences quickly.

I wanta go surfing.

I wanta go fishing.

I wanta go jogging.

I wanta go biking.

I wanta go kayaking.

Exercise 3 Repeat (listening)

When you speak slowly and clearly, you say "to." When you speak in normal conversation, you often say "ta."

Listen to and repeat these sentences slowly for practice.

I wanta play in the sand.
I wanta sit on the beach.
I wanta walk my dog.
I wanta walk on the beach.
I wanta go ta the beach.

Repeat (listening)

Now repeat these sentences quickly.

I wanta play in the sand.
I wanta sit on the beach.
I wanta walk my dog.
I wanta walk on the beach.
I wanta go ta the beach.

Exercise 4

However, saying "wanta" isn't the fastest way that it's pronounced. I often change the words "want to" to a single sound "wanna."

Listen

I wanna go surfing.
I wanna catch a wave.
I wanna ride a wave.
I wanna go golfing.
I wanna go camping.

Read

Now you try it, say these sentences quickly.

I wanna go surfing.
I wanna catch a wave.
I wanna ride a wave.
I wanna go golfing.
I wanna go camping.

Exercise 5 Read

Now, you change these sentences using "wanna."
Say them slowly.

I wanna go surfing.
I wanna go fishing.
I wanna go jogging.
I wanna go biking.
I wanna go kayaking.

Listen and Repeat

Now listen to these sentences and say them quickly.

I wanna go surfing.
I wanna go fishing.
I wanna go jogging.
I wanna go biking.
I wanna go kayaking.

Exercise 6 Repeat Slowly

Okay, so you understand the change. Listen to these sentences and see if you can understand and repeat them.

I wanna go ta the beach tamorrow.

I wanna take my family ta the beach.

I wanna go horseback riding taday.

I wanna walk in the water.

I wanna take a long walk on the beach.

Repeat

Here are some sentences, read them and change them for normal conversation.

I don't want to walk home.

Do you want to dance?

He doesn't want to come with us.

All I want to do is go home.

They want to stay at the beach all day.

Exercise 7 Present: Wants to

Here's one last change like this that you should know. When I say, "He wants to" I change "wants to" to "wansta."

Listen

He wansta play in the sand.

Read

He wansta play in the sand.

Listen and Repeat

Listen to these sentences and repeat them.

He wansta play in the sand.
He wansta learn to surf.
He wansta take his shoes off and run.
She wansta each her sandwich now.
It wansta steal your sandwich.

Read and Change

Last change these sentences using "wantsa."

He wants to go crabbing.

He wants to go biking.

He wants to go home.

He wants to sand his boat.

He wants to go boogey boarding.

Comment

"I live in a small town.

Do you wanna see it?"

One thing that you should understand: using "wanta" and "wanna" and "wansta" in conversation is perfectly fine when talking to friends. But these changes are almost never written. You should not write these changes in written letters, emails, or school papers, because these are spoken changes. They would look incorrect when written. So, in general, I don't write these.

And a last thing you should know: you must be able to use the formal English pronunciation when needed. You shouldn't just use the changes, "wanna" or "wansta" all the time.

When speaking to a friend, I might say, "I wanna go home."

But if this situation is formal or I need to speak clearly, I would say, "I want to go home." If I was in a meeting, I might say, "I wanna say something." But, if people didn't understand me, I'd slow down and say, "I want to say something." So in formal situations, you must be able to slow down and use formal pronunciation when needed.

Final Conversation

Okay, listen to this conversation for the changes that you've learned.

Hey, how's it going?

Pretty good, do you wanna see a movie tonight?

Sure, what do you wanna see?

Well, my girl friend is coming and she wansta see Avatar.

I already saw that, I don't wanna see it again.

Okay, good lesson, let's learn some more.

Lesson 2: To Into Onto   Of   Out Of

Introduction

In the last lesson you learned that the word "to" is often pronounced "ta" in casual conversation. In this lesson you'll learn that this common change is used in other words as well, for example, in the word "onto" and "into" and in the words "of" and "out of." This next lesson will present these changes to you and you'll get to practice them as well.

Exercise 1 Present: To

When I speak quickly, I often pronounce the word "to" as "ta." For example, I say, "I go ta the grocery store ta buy food." Listen to this change.

Listen

I go ta the café ta get coffee.

Read

I go ta the café ta get coffee.

Okay, let's practice this change until you're comfortable with it.

Exercise 2 Listen

Listen to these examples.

He went ta the library ta get a book.

He went ta McDonalds to get a burger.

He went ta the post office ta get stamps.

Go ta school ta get an education.

Break the law, go ta jail.

Read and Repeat

For practice read these sentences slowly and change "to" to "ta."

He went ta the library ta get a book.

He went ta McDonalds to get a burger.

He went ta the post office ta get stamps.

Go ta school ta get an education.

Break the law, go ta jail.

Now read these sentences quickly as you might say them in conversation.

He went ta the library ta get a book.

He went ta McDonalds to get a burger.

He went ta the post office ta get stamps.

Go ta school ta get an education.

Break the law, go ta jail.

Exercise 3 Read

Repeat these sentences quickly.

I went ta the movies.
I went ta the store.
I went ta the park.
I went ta the city.
I went ta school.

Repeat these sentences quickly.

I need to buy a book today.
I went to my friend's house.
Tomorrow, I go to work.
I go to school in the city.
I need to learn to stay calm.

Exercise 4 Present: into onto

The word "to" also changes to "ta" in the words "into" and "onto."

I went "inta" the store.

Did you hear it? I went "inta" the store. And,

I put the book "onta" the table.

Listen for the change"

I put the hat onta the table.

Listen

Now listen to these examples.

He put the envelope inta the fire.
He put the envelope inta the mailbox.
He put the book inta the box.
He put the book onta the table.
He put the magazine onta the stairs.

Exercise 5 Read and Repeat

Now read these sentences first slowly, then read them quickly changing the "to" sound to "ta."

He put the envelope into the fire.

He put the envelope into the mailbox.

He put the book into the box.

He put the book onto the table.

He put the magazine onto the stairs.

Read and Change

Read these sentences and change them to say them quickly.

I went into the store to buy a shirt.

I got into the car to go home.

She got onto the bus to go to work.

He wants to get onto a soccer team.

Let's go on to new things.

Exercise 6 Present: Of

And here's another small change, the word "of" is often pronounced quickly as "a." For example, "a box of crayons" is spoken as "a box a crayons."

Listen

A bowl of apples. A bowl a apples.
I put a bottle of water into the box. I put a bottle a water inta the box.

Exercise 7 Repeat (reading)

Now read and repeat these short phrases quickly for practice.

A pair a shoes.

A pair a boots.

A glass a juice.

A bottle a cider.

A basket a stuffed animals.

Repeat (listening)

Remember you must be able to use these change correctly. You must be able to say the phrases slowly and also use the changes when speaking quickly. Try this, first say the phrase slowly and then say it a quickly, changing "of" to "a."

A pair of shoes.

A pair of boots.

A glass of juice.

A bottle of cider.

A basket of stuffed animals.

Exercise 8 Present: Out of

Here's another little change. Instead of saying "out of" in conversation, I say "outa." For example, "They came outa the bakery." Can you hear the change?

Listen

They came outa the bakery.

Read

They came outa the bakery.

Listen

Listen to these examples.

He took the mail outa the box.
She took some crackers outa the box.
She took a drink outa the bottle.
He took his keys outa his pocket.

Repeat (reading)

Try reading and changing these sentences using "outa."

He took the mail outa the box.

She took some crackers outa the box.

She took a drink outa the bottle.

He took his keys outa his pocket.

Exercise 9 Listen and Repeat

Listen to these sentence spoken slowly, then you repeat them speeding them up.

I got out of my car.

She came out of the store.

The car came out of the parking lot.

She got out of school early.

She can't get out of bed.

Listen, Read, Repeat

Okay, let's practice a little by listening to sentences, reading the sentences, then speaking the sentences quickly.

He got out of the car to talk to her.

He went into the house to talk to her.

He got onto the train to go to work.

She got a bottle of water to take to work.

The car was out of gas.

Comment

"Notice there are a lota apples on that tree."

And notice that I said, "a lota." The word "of" often changes in many combination words, for example, with the words "kind of," "sort of," "a couple of," and "a lot of." All of these words sound with the "a" sound.

"Here's a buncha bananas."

"a cupa water for tea"

This is a very common change. Notice this change in normal conversation and try to make the change yourself as you speak.

Final Conversation

Okay, listen for the changes you've learned.

Hi! Are we goin ta the movies tanight?

Sure, I got a couple a tickets online.

Great, I wanna get outa here. I'm bored.

Does Sally wanna come?

Na, not tanight, she wansta, but she's has ta work tamorrow.

Lesson 3: Going to

Introduction

It's a nice day. She's gunna take a walk in the park.
She's gunna walk with her kids.

Can you hear the change? When I spoke quickly, I said, "She's gunna take a walk in the park. She's gunna take a walk."

The words "going to" are pronounced "gunna." When I need to speak clearly and be understood, I say, "She's going to walk in the park." But when I speak to a friend or informally, I say, "She's gunna. She's gunna walk in the park." You'll often hear this common change made in conversations.

Let's look closer at this change.

Listen

She's gunna stop on the bridge.

Read

She's gunna stop on the bridge.
He's gunna clean the sidewalk.
She's gunna pick him up.

Exercise 1 Repeat (reading)

For practice, read these sentences slowly out loud.

I'm gunna go ta the mall.

I'm gunna go shopping.

I'm gunna eat at the mall.

I'm gunna sweep the sidewalk.

I'm gunna sweep the porch.

Repeat (reading)

Now read these sentences out loud quickly.

I'm gunna go ta the mall.

I'm gunna go shopping.

I'm gunna eat at the mall.

I'm gunna sweep the sidewalk.

I'm gunna sweep the porch.

Exercise 2 Repeat (listening)

Listen to and repeat these sentences slowly for practice.

I'm gunna get in my car.

I'm gunna open the trunk.

I'm gunna get outa my car.

I'm gunna turn on the TV.

I'm gunna vacuum the rug.

Repeat (listening)

Now repeat these sentences quickly.

I'm gunna get in my car.

I'm gunna open the trunk.

I'm gunna get outa my car.

I'm gunna turn on the TV.

I'm gunna vacuum the rug.

Exercise 3 Listen

Now listen to these sentences spoken quickly.

She's gunna get some money from an ATM.

She's gunna go up the escalator.

He's gunna go upstairs.

He's gunna pass me.

He's gunna try some Chinese food.

Read

Now you try saying these sentences quickly.

She's going to get some money from an ATM.

She's going to go up the escalator.

He's going to go upstairs.

He's going to pass me.

He's going to try some Chinese food.

Exercise 4 Repeat (listening)

Now listen to these sentences and say them quickly.

He's gunna eat dinner.

She's gunna have a vacation.

She's gunna go home.

He's gunna see a movie.

We're gunna get a hamburger.

Repeat Slow (listening)

Okay, so you understand the change. Listen to these sentences and see if you can understand and repeat them slowly. Say the complete pronunciation as if you were speaking clearly to someone.

They're gunna get in the car and leave.

They're gunna play tennis all day.

They're gunna go shopping at the mall.

They gunna stop and watch the ducks.

They're gunna take a walk in the park.

Exercise 5 Repeat

Now, read these sentences and change them for normal conversation.

I'm going to walk home.

Are you going to go dancing?

He isn't going to come with us.

All I'm going to do is go home.

They're going go to the beach.

Okay, answer these questions using "gunna."

What are you gunna do? I'm gunna go ta the mall.

Where are you going?   Go shopping.

Where are you gunna eat? Eat at the mall.

What are you gunna do now? Sweep the sidewalk.

What are you gunna do next? Sweep the porch.

Final Conversation

Okay, listen to this conversation for the changes that you've learned.

Hi, what's up?

I'm gunna have a party on Friday. You wanna come?

Sorry, I can't, I wanna, but I'm gunna be visiting my grandma.

Are you gunna be there all weekend?

Yeah, we're gunna paint her house. She wansta paint it purple.

Lesson 4: You Are you?

Introduction

Listen to this: "Do ya wanna walk in the park?"

Did you hear the change? First you probably heard "wanna" in "Do you wanna walk in the park?" But did ya hear the change to the word "you"? Did ya?

Do ya wanna walk in the park?

This is an incredibly simple and common change. "You" changes to "ya."

Ya ready to learn it?

Let's look closer at this common change, listen.

Listen

I'll see ya at the park.

Read

I'll see ya at the park.

Exercise 1 Repeat (reading)

For practice, read these sentences slowly.
(Remember you almost never write these changes, the sentences you see here are just to help your practice saying them.)

I'll see ya later.
I'll see ya in an hour.
I'll see ya in a minute.
I'll see ya tanight.
I'll see ya tamorrow.

Repeat (reading)

Now say these sentences quickly.

I'll see ya later.
I'll see ya in an hour.
I'll see ya in a minute.
I'll see ya tanight.
I'll see ya tamorrow.

Exercise 2 Repeat (listening)

When I speak slowly and clearly, I say "you." When I speak in a normal conversation, I often say "ya."

Read and repeat these sentences slowly for practice.

I wanna show ya the park.
I wanna buy ya lunch.
I wanna buy ya some gas.
I wanna buy ya something ta eat.
I wanna buy ya a smoothie.

Repeat (listening)

Now repeat these sentences quickly.

I wanna show ya the park.
I wanna buy ya lunch.
I wanna buy ya some gas.
I wanna buy ya something ta eat.
I wanna buy ya a smoothie.

Exercise 3 Listen

You also change "you" to "ya" when asking simple questions.

Are ya gunna take a bus?

Are ya gunna get some gas?

Are ya gunna take the highway?

Are ya gunna park by the house?

Are ya gunna work outside?

Read

Now you try asking these questions.

Are ya gunna take a bus?

Are ya gunna get some gas?

Are ya gunna take the highway?

Are ya gunna park by the house?

Are ya gunna work outside?

Exercise 4 Read and Change

Now, change these questions using "ya" and "gunna."
Say them slowly.

Are you going to eat dinner?

Are you going to take a vacation?

Are you going to go home?

Are you going to see a movie?

Are you going to get a hamburger?

Repeat

Now listen to these sentences and say them quickly

Are ya gunna eat dinner?

Are ya gunna take a vacation?

Are ya gunna go home?

Are ya gunna see a movie?

Are ya gunna get a hamburger?

Exercise 5 Repeat Slow

Okay, so you understand the change. Listen to these sentences and see if you can understand and repeat them slowly.

I'll talk ta ya later.

She likes ya.

See ya tamorrow

Are ya gunna go now?

Do ya wanna dance?

Read and Change

Here are some sentences, read them and change them for normal conversation.

Are you going to walk home?

Do you have any money?

He doesn't like you much.

I want to take you to dinner.

Will you be home tomorrow?

Comment

One thing that you should understand. If you only use the word "ya" when you talk, you might sound uneducated. You must use the "ya" change at the right time. When speaking clearly or in formal situations, you'll usually say "you." For example, at work, you might say, "Will I see you at the meeting?"

But in situations with friends, I usually say, "Will I see ya at the restaurant?"

You must be able to use both pronunciations.

Final Conversation

Okay, listen to this conversation for the changes that you've learned.

Hey, how ya doing?

Ya know, I'm in a hurry. Are ya gunna go downtown, I need a ride?

Sure, I was gunna leave in a minute for work.

Great, I don't wanna be late taday.

Okay, see ya in a minute.

Review

Let's review the changes you've learned so far.

I'm going ta the store.

He went inta the store

He put it onta the table.

She came outa the house angry.

I wanna eat dinner.

She wansta see me.

I'll call ya later.

I'm gunna go home.

Do ya wanna dance?

Lesson 5 Jogging Are you?

Introduction

Look at Claire. She's gettun ready to jog. And now she's joggun slow.
Notice that I didn't say "getting ready", I said "gettun ready." And I didn't say
"jogging slow," I said "joggun slow."

I often change the sound from "ing" to "un" as I speak.

Listen

She's joggun slow.

Read

She's joggun slow.

This is a very common change in conversation. Let's practice it.

40

Exercise 1 Repeat (reading)

For practice, read and repeat these sentences slowly.

He's washun the dishes.

He's washun the windows.

He's washun the windshield.

He's cleanun the mirror.

He's cleanun the rug.

Repeat (reading)

Now read these sentences quickly.

He's washun the dishes.

He's washun the windows.

He's washun the windshield.

He's cleanun the mirror.

He's cleanun the rug.

Exercise 2 Repeat (listening)

For practice, read and repeat these sentences slowly.

He's writun a check.

He's puttun on a stamp.

He's payun a bill.

He's puttun it in the mailbox.

He's checkun for mail.

Repeat (listening)

Now repeat these same sentences quickly.

He's writun a check.

He's puttun on a stamp.

He's payun a bill.

He's puttun it in the mailbox.

He's checkun for mail.

Exercise 3 Repeat (listening)

Now listen to these sentences and repeat them slowly.

"He's waitun for food."

Notice that the word "for" is now pronounce "fer."

He's waitun fer food.
He's waitun fer a bus.
He's waitun fer class.
He's waitun fer a taxi.
He's waitun fer a friend.

Repeat (listening)

Now listen to these sentences and repeat them quickly. Be sure to say "fer" instead of "for."

He's waitun fer food.
He's waitun fer a bus.
He's waitun fer class.
He's waitun fer a taxi.
He's waitun fer a friend.

Exercise 4 Repeat (listening)

Let's try a few more examples. Listen to these sentences and repeat them slowly. Remember that the word "to" is now pronounce "ta."

I'm hopun ta see him.

I'm hopun ta go home soon.

I'm hopun ta catch a taxi.

I'm hopun ta see my friend.

I'm hopun ta leave work early.

Repeat (listening)

Now listen to these sentences and repeat them quickly.

I'm hopun ta see him.

I'm hopun ta go home soon.

I'm hopun ta catch a taxi.

I'm hopun ta see my friend.

I'm hopun ta leave work early.

Exercise 5 Repeat (reading)

Next read these sentences and then say them quickly using the change.

They're riding on the beach.

He's waiting by the ocean.

He's sitting and watching the ocean.

They're walking and enjoying the weather.

They're fishing and feeding the gulls.

Repeat (listening)

Try saying these sentences slowly without the change.

He's cleanun the counter.

He's cleanun the stove.

He's loadun the dishwasher.

He's goun fer a walk.

She's walkun on the pier.

Listen and Change

Now listen to these same sentence said slowly, and you repeat them quickly.

He's cleaning the counter.

He's cleaning the stove.

He's loading the dishwasher.

He's going for a walk.

She's walking on the pier.

Exercise 6 Present: Are you?

Before we finish this lesson, let's look at a change that I make when asking simple questions.

Ya ready? Ya listenun? You hearun it?

Instead of asking, "Are you listening?" I said, "Ya listenun?" "Ya listenun?" I dropped the question word "are."

Listen

Are you ready? Ya ready?
Are you hearing it? Ya hearun it?

Exercise 7 Listen

Listen to these questions.

Ya eatun dinner?

Ya goun home?

Ya walkun home?

She buyun that dress?

He workun taday?

Repeat (reading)

Now read these questions and shorten them as you might in conversation.

Are you eating dinner?

Are you going home?

Are you walking home?

Is she buying that dress?

Is he working today?

Read and Change

Now, read these questions and shorten them as you might in conversation.

Do you want to dance?

Have you seen Tom around?

Are you looking to buy a car?

Is she staying home?

Are you looking for something?

Exercise 8   Present: Aren't you?

A common way to ask politely about something is to ask using "Aren't you?"

For example, if I'm not sure that you're going to work, I might ask

Aren't you going to work?

And if I say it a little faster, I say

Aren't ya going to work? Aren't ya?

But, if I say it really quickly, I would say "arntcha?"

Arntcha going to work? Arntcha?

Listen

Arntcha going ta the movies?
Arntcha going home?
Arntcha gunna have dinner?
Arntcha gunna call her?
Arntcha gunna visit her?

Repeat these questions using Arntcha:

Arntcha going ta the movies?
Arntcha going home?
Arntcha gunna have dinner?
Arntcha gunna call her?
Arntcha gunna visit her?

Some people pronounce "Arntcha" slightly differently.
They say "Arntchew."

.

Arntchew going ta work?

You can say "Arntcha" or "Arntchew," it makes no difference.

For practice, ask these questions using "Arntchew."

Arntchew going ta the movies?
Arntchew going home?
Arntchew gunna have dinner?
Arntchew gunna call her?
Arntchew gunna visit her?

Comment

Remember that there are two speeds for speaking with changes. You must be able to speak clearly and slowly without the changes. And you can use the changes to speak quickly in casual conversation. You should not really use this pronunciation when speaking slowly. It can sound odd or maybe even uneducated if you do.

Final Conversation

Listen to this conversation and see if you can hear the changes that you've learned in this lesson.

Hi, ya home soon?

No, I'm workun late. I'm gunna be here fer another hour.

Ya want me to start cookun somethun?

Fer sure. I'm leavun as soon as I can.

Okay, I'll be waitun. Bye.

Lesson 6 Have to Has to Have Got to

Introduction

Hey, Claire ya commun?

Just a minute, I hafta find my keys!

What?

I hafta find my keys!

What?

I gotta find my keys!

In this lesson you'll learn two common changes: "I have to" and "I have got to."

Did you hear the change?

I hafta find my keys. I hafta.

Also, "I've got to" changes to "gotta."

I gotta find my keys.

Listen

I hafta find my keys.

I gotta find my keys.

Read

I hafta find my keys.

I gotta find my keys.

Exercise 1 Repeat (reading)

For practice, read these sentences slowly out loud.

I hafta buy some flowers.

I hafta buy a card.

I hafta buy a pen.

I hafta buy some staples.

I hafta buy some cat food.

Now read these same sentences again using "gotta."

I gotta buy some flowers.

I gotta buy a card.

I gotta buy a pen.

I gotta buy some staples.

I gotta buy some cat food.

Repeat (reading)

Now read these quickly

I hafta buy some flowers.

I hafta buy a card.

I hafta buy a pen.

I hafta buy some staples.

I hafta buy some cat food.

I gotta buy some flowers.

I gotta buy a card.

I gotta buy a pen.

I gotta buy some staples.

I gotta buy some cat food.

Exercise 2 Repeat (listening)

When you speak slowly and clearly, you say "have to" and "have got to."
When you speak in normal conversation, you often say "hafta" and "gotta."

Repeat these sentences slowly for practice.

I hafta practice the piano.
I hafta wash the clothes.
I hafta iron my shirt.
I gotta water the flowers.
I gotta take out the garbage.

Repeat (listening)

Now repeat these sentences quickly.

I hafta practice the piano.
I hafta wash the clothes.
I hafta iron my shirt.
I gotta water the flowers.
I gotta take out the garbage.

Exercise 3 Listen

Also, when saying "has to" as in the sentence "He has to go home," I often change the words "has to" to "hasta."

She hasta do her homework.
She hasta practice the piano.
He hasta buy some new bananas.
He hasta buy some more cereal.
He hasta get some exercise.

Read

Now you try it.

She hasta do her homework.
She hasta practice the piano.
He hasta buy some new bananas.
He hasta buy some more cereal.
He hasta get some exercise.

Exercise 4 Read and Change

Now, you change these sentences using "hafta" and "gotta."
Say them slowly.

I have to eat dinner.

I've got to have a vacation.

I have to leave early.

I've got to make a phone call.

I have to get my work done.

Repeat (listening)

Now listen to these sentences and say them quickly

I halfta eat dinner.

I gotta have a vacation.

I halfta leave early.

I gotta make a phone call.

I halfta get my work done.

Exercise 5 Repeat

Okay, so you understand the changes. Listen to these sentences and see if you can understand and repeat them.

I gotta go for a walk tamorrow.
I hafta get up early and go golfun.
I gotta go ta that new restaurant.
I gotta see this new movie.
I hafta work all day taday.

Read and Change

Here are some sentences, read them out loud slowly, then change them for normal conversation.

I have to walk home.
Do you have to stay here long?
He doesn't have to come with us.
I've just got to go home.
He has to work this weekend.

Comment

So here the words "have got to" are pronounced as a single word "gotta."
One thing that you should understand is that when asking a question you start it with "have:"

Have you got to stay long?

Have ya gotta stay long?

You never say, "Do you gotta stay long?"
Instead you say "Do you hafta stay long?"

And when using he or she, you say "He's gotta," "She's gotta."

Listen
He's gotta get a new car.
She's gotta buy groceries.
He's gotta go home after work.
She's gotta babysit tanight.

Repeat
Read and repeat these sentences quickly changing them for conversation.
He's got to get a new car.
She's got to buy groceries.
He's got to go home after work.
She's got to babysit tonight.

Final Conversation

Okay, listen to this conversation for the changes that you've learned.

Morning. I gotta go ta work early.

Why? Do ya hafta do somethun special?

Yeah, I hafta finish a report fer my boss.

I thought Cheryl was gunna do the report?

She was, but, she got sick and hasta stay home.

Okay, good lesson, let's learn some more.

Lesson 7: Do You?

Introduction

Here's Claire. She's gunna run the 10K.
Do you wanna run the 10K?

Now listen to this simple question. I'm going to say it four times. Each time I'm going to say it slightly faster. Listen for the changes I make.

Do you want to run the 10K?
Do ya wanna run the 10K?
Dya wanna run the 10K?
Ya wanna run the 10K?

First, I spoke slowly and clearly as anyone would in a formal situation.

Do you want to run the 10K?

Then I spoke a little quicker, using "ya" and "wanna."

Do ya wanna run the 10K?

The next time I asked it, I made a small change, instead of saying Do ya, I said "Dya."

Dya

Dya wanna run the 10K?

And last, in a very informal way, I just dropped the question word "do" entirely.

Ya wanna run the 10K?

In this lesson you'll make these changes to simple questions that use "do."

Listen

Do ya like ta run?
Dya like ta run?
Ya like ta run?

Read

Do ya like ta run?
Dya like ta run?
Ya like ta run?

Exercise 1 Repeat (reading)

For practice, read these sentences slowly.

Do ya wanna have an orange?

Do ya wanna have some orange juice?

Do ya wanna have some milk?

Do ya wanna have some tea?

Do ya wanna have a nap?

Dya wanna have an orange?

Dya wanna have some orange juice?

Dya wanna have some milk?

Dya wanna have some tea?

Dya wanna have a nap?

Repeat (reading)

Now read these quickly.

Do ya wanna have an orange?

Do ya wanna have some orange juice?

Do ya wanna have some milk?

Do ya wanna have some tea?

Do ya wanna have a nap?

Dya wanna have an orange?

Dya wanna have some orange juice?

Dya wanna have some milk?

Dya wanna have some tea?

Dya wanna have a nap?

Exercise 2 Repeat (listening)

When you speak slowly and clearly, you say "Do you." When you speak in normal conversation, you often say "Do ya" and "Dya."

Listen and repeat these questions for practice.

Do ya see her?
Do ya see her number?
Do ya see her now?
Do ya see her at the starting line?
Do ya see her coming?

Repeat (listening)

Now repeat these sentences quickly using "Dya."

Dya see her?
Dya see her number?
Dya see her now?
Dya see her at the starting line?
Dya see her coming?

Exercise 3 Listen

Now, for practice, listen and repeat these questions using to the very short informal form "ya."

Ya see her?

Ya see her number?

Ya see her at the start?

Ya see her comun?

Read

Now you try it, change these questions using "Ya."

Do you want to eat dinner?

Do you want to see a movie?

Do you want to go home?

Do you have to stay late?

Do you want to eat something?

Exercise 4 Read and Change

Now, you change these questions using "Do ya" or "Dya."
Say them slowly.

Do you need something?
Do you want to stay here?
Do you have to get up early?
Do you have a car?
Do you think he's coming?

Repeat (listening)

Now listen to these questions and say them quickly using "Dya." Then say them again using just "Ya."

For example:

Dya have any money? Ya have any money?

Now you try it.

Dya need somethun?
Dya want to stay here?
Dya have to get up early?
Dya have a car?
Dya think he's comun?

66

Exercise 5 Repeat (reading)

Okay, say these questions four ways, with "Do you," then "Do ya," then "Dya," and finally with "Ya." Like this:

Do you want to have lunch?

Do ya wanna have lunch?

Dya wanna have lunch?

Ya wanna have lunch?

Do you want to walk to school?   Do ya?   Dya?   Ya?

Do you have to get up early?

Do you want to go to the movies?

Do you need to get gas?

Do you have to work tomorrow?

Exercise 6 Present: Does He? Does She?

Let's look at two small changes like this. When I ask a question like:
Does he like to run?

I often shorten it to sound like this:
Dzi like ta run?

I say, Dzi. Dzi. Dzi like ta run?

And when I ask,

Does she like to run?

I often shorten it to sound like this,

Dshi like ta run?
Dshi. Dshi. Dshi like ta run?

Listen
Dzi like ta run?
Dzshi like ta run?

Read
Dzi like ta run?
Dzshi like ta run?

Exercise 7 Repeat and Change (reading)

For practice read these sentences and change them to say them quickly.

Does he have a car?

Does he need money?

Does he read much?

Does he like music?

Does she dance well?

Does she go to school?

Does she have a job?

Does she like me?

Comment

A common way to ask politely about something is to ask using "Don't you?"

For example, if I'm not sure you like pop music, I might ask

Don't you like pop music?

And if I say it a little faster, I say

Don't ya like pop music? Don't ya?

But, if I say it really quickly, I would change it to say

"Dontcha"

Dontcha like pop music?

Listen

Dontcha like old movies?
Dontcha have any money?
Dontcha have a job?
Dontcha need more money?
Dontcha have a car?

Repeat these questions using Dontcha:

Dontcha like old movies?

Dontcha have any money?

Dontcha have a job?

Dontcha need more money?

Dontcha have a car?

Some people pronounce Dontcha slightly differently.

They say "Dontchew"

.

Dontchew like pop music?

You can say Dontcha or Dontchew, it makes no difference.

For practice, a
sk these questions using Dontchew.

Don't you like my hat?

Don't you like old movies?

Don't you have any money?

Don't you speak English?

Don't you want to dance?

Final Conversation

Listen to this conversation for the changes that you've learned.

Hi. Dya wanna come over?

Sure, ya havun a party?

No, just a couple a friends.

Dya want me ta bring you some pizza?

Dya think ya could? That'd be great!

Lesson 8: Will you?   Won't you?   When will you?

Introduction

In this lesson, you'll learn a little more about asking questions. You'll hear simple questions spoken with common changes. We'll start with easy ones first.

You'll learn how to change these questions.

Will you?
Won't you?
When will you?

Let's get started.

You can easily hear this change.

Will you come home soon? Willya come home soon?

"Will you" becomes, "'Will ya."
Willya have dinner with me?
Willya need money?

This is easy, because you've used "ya" instead of "you" before. Practice this a little.

Listen

Will you rent a car?
Willya rent a car?

Read

Willya rent a car?

Exercise 1 Repeat (reading)

For practice, say these sentences slowly.

Willya come early?

Willya come late?

Willya come soon?

Willya come on time?

Willya come later?

Repeat (reading)

Now ask the questions quickly.

Willya come early?

Willya come late?

Willya come soon?

Willya come on time?

Willya come later?

Repeat (listening)

For practice say these questions quickly.

Will you have dinner with us?

Will you stay a while?

Will you stay for lunch?

Will you give me your phone number?

Will you go there with me?

Exercise 2 Present: Won't you?

Now the polite way of inviting someone to do something uses "Won't you?"

For example, if I want a friend to have dinner with me, I say,

"Won't you have dinner with me?"

But because it's my friend, I'd say it faster. I'd say,

Wontya have dinner with me? Wontya.
Wontya have dinner with me?

Listen to these questions for the change.

Wontya have dinner with me?
Wontya stay a while?
Wontya stay fer lunch?
Wontya call me?
Wontya come with me?

Now, listen to this final change when I ask these questions very quickly.

Wontcha have dinner with us?
Wontcha stay a while?
Wontcha stay fer lunch?
Wontcha call me?

Wontcha come with me?

Did you hear it? "Wontya" changed to "wontcha" "wontcha."

In this case because the word wont ends in a T, the word "you" changes to "cha" "Wontcha?"

You'll hear this change again in other lessons to come.

Exercise 3 Listen and Read

Now ask these questions quickly using "wantya."

Wontya be late?

Wontya be tired?

Wontya be cold?

Wontya be nervous?

Wontya be hot?

Now ask these questions again using "wonthca."

Wontcha be late?

Wontcha be tired?

Wontcha be cold?

Wontcha be nervous?

Wontcha be hot?

Exercise 4 Read and Change

Now, change these questions using "ya."

Won't you eat dinner with us?

Won't you come for a visit?

Won't you stay longer?

Won't you sing for us?

Won't you need more money?

Now ask these questions using "wontcha."

Won't you eat dinner with us?

Won't you come for a visit?

Won't you stay longer?

Won't you sing for us?

Won't you need more money?

Exercise 5 Repeat

Okay, so you understand the change. Listen to these questions and see if you can understand and repeat them slowly.

Willya come to the party?

Wontcha need a reservation?

Wontya need more money?

Willya have a cookie?

Wontcha need a hat?

Repeat (reading)

Now read the same questions and say them quickly with the changes you've learned.

Will you come to the party?

Won't you need a reservation?

Won't you need more money?

Will you have a cookie?

Won't you need a hat?

Exercise 6 Present: When will you? How will you?

Now let's learn a last simple change that you may already know. When you ask a question such as, "When will you come home?"
the words "will" changes to a "ul" sound.   Here listen:

When will you come home? Whenlya come home?

Did you hear it?

Whenlya whenlya

When will you come home? Whenlya?

Listen

Whenlya come home?
Whenlya be here?
Howlya get to work?
Whatlya buy when ya get there?

Read

Whenlya come home?
Whenlya be here?
Howlya get to work?
Whatlya buy when ya get there?

81

Listen and Change

Now change these questions saying them quickly.

How will you get there?

When will you get there?

What will you buy there?

Who will you see there?

Why will you go there?

Comment

Just so you know, some people may pronounce "wontcha" differently. They may say "wontchew."

Wontchew stay with us? Wontchew?

"Wontchew" and "wontcha" are used the same. It makes no difference.

Wontchew be tired?
Wontcha be tired?
Wontchew be late?
Wontcha be late?

So know that you can say "wontchew" or "wontcha" and it makes no difference. The person you're talking to probably won't even notice.

Final Conversation

Okay, listen to this conversation for the changes that you've learned.

Hi, Will ya be home late tanight?

I don't know, I gotta do a lot a work here.

Wontcha try to be here on time? I'm cookun a nice dinner.

Whenlya have it ready?

About 7.

Okay, I'll finish up and get home soon.

Will ya? Great thanks.

Lesson 9: What are you?

Introduction

Well, you're doing great. Now listen to this question. I'm going to say it four times. Each time I'm going to say it slightly faster. Listen to the changes I make.

What are you doing?
Whataya doun?
Whatya doun?
Whatcha doun?

First, I spoke slowly and clearly as anyone would in a formal situation. What are you doing?

Then I spoke a little quicker, using "aya." Instead of saying "What are you," I said "Whataya."

Whataya doun? Whataya doun?

In the next change, I dropped the "are" sound entirely, and said Whatya

What are you doing?
Whatya doun?

And last, in a very informal way, I changed "ya" to "cha."

What are you doing?
Whatcha doun?

In this lesson you'll make these changes to simple questions that use "are you."

Listen

What are you doing?
Whataya doun?
Whatya doun?
Whatcha doun?

Read

What are you doing?
Whataya doun?
Whatya doun?
Whatcha doun?

Exercise 1 Repeat (reading)

For practice, read these questions slowly using "whataya."

Whataya doun?

Whataya makun?

Whataya eatun?

Whataya drinkun?

Whataya buyun?

Now ask these same questions slowly using "whatya."

Whatya doun?

Whatya makun?

Whatya eatun?

Whatya drinkun?

Whatya buyun?

Now say these sentences again using "whatcha."

Whatcha doun?

Whatcha makun?

Whatcha eatun?

Whatcha drinkun?

Whatcha buyun?

Repeat (reading)

Now that you've had some practice ask these questions quickly.

Whataya doun?

Whataya makun?

Whataya eatun?

Whataya drinkun?

Whataya buyun?

Whatya doun?

Whatya makun?

Whatya eatun?

Whatya drinkun?

Whatya buyun?

Whatcha doun?

Whatcha makun?

Whatcha eatun?

Whatcha drinkun?

Whatcha have in the box?

Exercise 2 Repeat (listening)

When you speak slowly and clearly, you say "What are you." When you speak in normal conversation, you often say "Whataya."

Repeat these sentences slowly for practice.

Whataya havun fer breakfast?
Whataya makun fer lunch?
Whataya lookun for?
Whataya doun with that?
Whataya havun fer lunch?

Repeat fast (listening)

Now repeat these sentences quickly using "whataya."

Whataya havun fer breakfast?
Whataya makun fer lunch?
Whataya lookun for?
Whataya doun with that?
Whataya havun fer lunch?

Exercise 3 Listen

Now, for practice, change these questions to the very short informal form, "Whatya."

Whatya havun fer breakfast?

Whatya makun fer lunch?

Whatya lookun for?

Whatya doun with that?

Whatya havun fer lunch?

Read

Now you try it even faster, change these questions using "cha."

What are you having for breakfast?

What are you making for lunch?

What are you looking for?

What are you doing with that?

What are you having for lunch?

Exercise 4 Read and Change

Now, you change these sentences using "whataya."

What are you going to buy?

What are you going to drink?

What are you going to listen to?

What are you going to fix?

Listen and Change

Now listen to these sentences and say them quickly using "Whatya."

Whatya gunna buy?

Whatya gunna drink?

Whatya gunna listen to?

Whatya gunna fix?

Repeat

Now use the shorted form of the question "cha," a very informal form.

Whatcha gunna buy?

Whatcha gunna drink?

Whatcha gunna listen to?

Whatcha gunna fix?

Exercise 5 Read and Change

Okay, so you understand the changes. Listen to these questions asked four
ways, formally, with "aya," with "ya," and finally use "cha." Like this:

What are you doing?

Whataya doun?

Whatya doun?

Whatcha doun?

What are you watching? Whataya? Whatya?   Whatcha?

What are you going to buy?

What are you talking about?

What are you going to do?

What are you thinking about?

Final Conversation

Okay, listen to this conversation for the changes you've learned.

Hey, whatcha doun?

Oh, just checkun my account.

Whataya gunna buy? Somethun expensive?

Oh, just a birthday present fer my friend. I wanna get her something special.

Whatdya gunna buy? Jewelry?

I wanna buy her a nice bracelet.

Lesson 10 When are you? Why are you? How are you? What time are you?

Introduction

Okay I want to know when my friend is going to the hardware store. So I call him up and say,

Hey, Tom, whenaya goun ta the hardware store?

Formally, I would have said,

Hi, Tom, when are you going to the hardware store?

But to a friend, I shorten it and say it quickly.

Whenaya goun ta the hardware store?

I asked, "Whenaya."

Whenaya gunna come over?

Listen

Whenaya gunna buy a new car?

Whenaya gunna buy a new car?

Read

Whenaya gunna buy a new car?

Exercise 1 Repeat (reading)

For practice, read these sentences slowly to yourself.

Whenaya gunna buy a car?

Whenaya gunna buy one?

Whenaya gunna buy more?

Whenaya gunna buy a ticket?

Whenaya gunna buy it?

Repeat (reading)

Now read these questions quickly.

Whenaya gunna buy a car?

Whenaya gunna buy one?

Whenaya gunna buy more?

Whenaya gunna buy a ticket?

Whenaya gunna buy it?

Exercise 2 Repeat (listening)

Read and repeat these sentences slowly for practice.

Whenaya takun a vacation?

Whenaya leavun?

Whenaya goun ta ballet class?

Whenaya goun skatun?

Whenaya gunna iron that shirt?

Repeat (listening)

Now ask these questions quickly.

Whenaya takun a vacation?

Whenaya leavun?

Whenaya goun ta ballet class?

Whenaya goun skatun?

Whenaya gunna iron that shirt?

Exercise 3   Listen

However, saying "whenaya" isn't the fastest way that I pronounce it. I often change the words "whenaya" to a single sound "whenya."

Listen to these examples.

Whenya goun ta the store?
Whenya goun ta the toy store?
Whenya goun ta the hardware store?
Whenya goun ta the grocery store?
Whenya gunna get a smoothie?

Read

Now you try asking these questions using "whenya."

Whenya goun ta the store?
Whenya goun ta the toy store?
Whenya goun ta the hardware store?
Whenya goun ta the grocery store?
Whenya gunna get a smoothie?

Exercise 4   Listen

Read and Change.

Now, you ask these questions using "whenya."
Say them quickly.

Whenya wanna eat dinner?

Whenya wanna go shopping?

Whenya wanna go home?

Whenya wanna see the movie?

Whenya wanna come over?

Repeat

Okay, so you understand the change. Listen to these sentences and see if you can understand and repeat them slowly.

Whenaya comun home from work?

Whenaya gunna get up fer work?

Whenya thinkun a comun?

Whenya gunna call her?

Whenya havun dinner?

Exercise 5 Present: How are you? Why are you? What time are you?

You've learned that when asking questions in conversation, "are you" often becomes the sound "aya." This change works with other question words as well, for example, how, where, why, and what time. But most often, question words like how, where, why, what time are spoken in the shortest form.

How are you going to get there?
Howya gunna get there?

Where are you going?
Whereya goun?

What time are you going to arrive?
What timeya gonna arrive?

Repeat

Listen to these questions and repeat them

Howya gunna get home?
Whyya gunna leave now?
What timeya hafta leave?
Whatya gunna do after work?
Whereya gunna park your car?

Read and Change

Change these sentences to speak them quickly. Use the short forms of "Howya," "Whyya," "What timeya," "Whereya."

How are you going to get home?

Why have you got to leave now?

What time do you have to leave?

What are you going to do after work?

Where are you going to park your car?

Comment

If you listen, you'll hear the changes that you're learning here in popular music.

Here, listen to a small part of this old song by The Beach Boys.

"Do ya, do ya, do ya, do ya wanna dance?"
"Do ya, do ya, do ya, do ya wanna dance?"
"Do ya, do ya, do ya, do ya, do you wanna dance?"

Years later old songs are forgotten. But the changes that you're learning here are not. The changes are spoken everyday, and will be used for many many years to come.

Final Conversation

Okay, listen to this conversation for the changes that you've learned.

Hi, what timeya comun over?

Oh, a little later. I gotta walk.

Whyya gunna walk?

My car's in the shop. No choice.

Whatcha gunna do if it rains?

I'm gunna get wet.

Lesson 11 What do you? When do you? Why do you?

Introduction

Let's continue practicing simple questions in the present. In this lesson you'll ask simple questions using:

What do you?
When do you?
Why do you?

Youve learned that instead of saying "Do you" in question you can use the sound "Dya." "Dya take the bus?" You'll practice using this same sound when asking What, When, and Why questions.

Whendya take the bus?

Let's get started.

Exercise 1 Present: What do you?

Listen to these examples of simple questions that use "Do you."

What do you have to buy?
Whadya hafta buy?

When do you have to be there?
Whendya hafta be there?

Why do you have to fix the roof?
Whydya hafta fix the roof?

"What do you" changes to "whadya."

Whadya   Whadya hafta buy?

"When do you" changes to "whendya."

Whendya Whendya hafta be there?

"Why do you" changes to "whydya."

Whydya   Whydya hafta fix the roof?

Listen

Whadya hafta buy?
Whendya hafta buy it?
Whydya hafta buy one?

Read

Whadya hafta buy?
Whendya hafta buy it?
Whydya hafta buy one?

Exercise 2 Repeat (reading)

For practice, say these sentences slowly.

Whadya wanna buy?

Whadya wanna get?

Whendya wanna go riding?

Whendya hafta mow the lawn?

Whydya want raspberries?

Whydya hafta fix the roof?

Repeat (reading)

Now read it quickly.

Whadya wanna buy?

Whadya wanna get?

Whendya wanna go riding?

Whendya hafta mow the lawn?

Whydya want raspberries?

Whydya hafta fix the roof?

Exercise 3 Repeat (listening)

Listen to these questions spoken quickly, then repeat them speaking slowly and clearly.
For example, make this change.

Whadya have in your hand?
What do you have in your hand?

Now you try it. Repeat these questions slowly for practice.

Whadya hafta do at work taday?
Whendya hafta go to work?
Whendya wanna eat lunch?
Whydya wanna use my phone?
Whydya wanna talk ta her?

Repeat (listening)

Now repeat these sentences quickly.

What do you have in your hand?
What do you have to do at work?
When do you have to go to work?
When do you want to eat lunch?
Why do you want to use my phone?
Why do you want to talk to her?

Exercise 4 Present: What do you?

Saying "Whadya" isn't the fastest way that it's pronounced. I often change the words "Whadya" to a single sound "Whatya."

Whatya wanna do?

It's the same with "When do you" and "Why do you." You can shorten them to,

Whenya   Whenya wanna go home?
Whya   Whya wanna go home?

Listen

Whatya wanna buy now?
Whatya need ta do?
Whenya hafta leave?
Whenya wanna buy one?
Whya hafta go now?

Read

Now you try it, ask these questions slowly using the changes for practice.

Whatya wanna buy now?
Whatya need ta do?

Whenya hafta leave?

Whenya wanna buy one?

Whya hafta go now?

Read and Change

Now, you say these sentences quickly using "Whatya," "Whenya," and "Whyya."

What do you want to buy now?

What do you need to do?

When do you have to leave?

When do you want to buy one?

Why do you have to go now?

Exercise 5 Review: What do you?

You've learned to say,

What do you
Whadya
Whatya

And you can also shorten "Whatya" to say, "Whatcha."

Whatcha wanna do?
Whatcha wanna buy?
Whatcha need ta get?

Let's briefly practice asking questions with "Whatcha."

Read to these questions and change them to use "Whatcha."

What are you going to buy?
What do you want to buy?
What are you doing?
What do you have to do?
What are you looking for?

Read and Change

Change these questions to speak them quickly using "Whadya," "Whendya," "Whydya."

What do you do at work?

Why do you have to be there early?

When do you get home from work?

What do you want to do tomorrow?

When do you have to leave?

Comment: What are you? What do you?

You've learned that you can say "Whataya" instead of "What are you." You can also say "Whadya" instead of "What do you."

What are you going to do?
Whataya gunna do?
What do you want to do?
Whadya wanna do?

In informal conversation, you can say "Whataya" and "Whadya" for the same question. It's kind of a question word that means the same thing.

Whataya gunna do?
Whadya gunna do?

They mean the same and sound nearly the same.

So if you say, "Whataya wanna do" or "Whadya wanna do" in informal conversation, no one will likely notice the difference. You would never write this. It is very informal. And when you speak slowly and clearly, you would say, "What are you" or "What do you."

Whataya gunna buy?
Whadya gunna buy?

Read and Change

For practice, say these sentences using both "Whataya" and "Whadya."

Whataya wanna do?

Whataya gunna buy now?

Whataya thinkun a doun now?

Whataya havun fer lunch?

Whataya gunna do now?

Final Conversation

Okay, listen to this conversation for the changes that you've learned.

Hi, Whatcha doun?

Nothun much. Whya askun?

Oh, I wanna go ta the movies.

Okay, gotcha. Whenya wanna go?

Right now.

Okay, I'll be there in a coupla minutes.

Lesson 12   Can Can you? When can you?

Introduction

"Hi. Kinya join me for a walk on the beach?"

Next, let's listen to another small pronunciation change. It's a change to the word "can."

First, I'll say a sentence with "can" slowly and clearly.
 Come on. I can show you the beach.

Now I'm going to speed it up slightly.
Come on. I kin show ya the beach.

When I said it quickly, I said "kin" instead of "can." Listen.

Come on. I kin show ya the beach.

Listen
I kin show ya the beach.
I kin show ya the beach.

Read

I kin show ya the beach.

Exercise 1 Repeat (reading)

For practice, read these sentences slowly changing "can" to "kin."

I kin come later.

I kin come now.

I kin come in an hour.

I kin come in a little while

I kin come in five minutes.

Repeat (reading)

Now read these sentences out loud quickly.

I kin come later.

I kin come now.

I kin come in an hour.

I kin come in a little while

I kin come in five minutes.

Exercise 2 Repeat (listening)

When you speak slowly and clearly, you say "can." When you speak in normal conversation, you often say "kin."

Listen to these sentences spoken quickly and you repeat them speaking slowly and clearly.

I kin see people on the beach.
I kin see him walkun on the beach.
I kin see them talkun on the beach.
You kin see a lota gulls on the beach.
She kin see a lota gulls on the beach.

Repeat (listening)

Now listen and repeat these sentences saying them quickly.

I kin see people on the beach.
I kin see him walkun on the beach.
I kin see them talkun on the beach.
You kin see a lota gulls on the beach.
She kin see a lota gulls on the beach.

Exercise 3 Present: Can you

You can also use this change when you ask questions using "can." For example, listen to this question asked slowly and then asked quickly.

Can you see the rabbit?

Kinya see the rabbit?

Kinya see the rabbit?

"Can you" changes to "Kinya' when spoken quickly.

Listen

Kinya see two rabbits?

Kinya see the raven in the grass?

Kinya see the hawk in the grass?

Kinya see the hawk on the fence?

Kinya see the gull by the bench?

Read

Now you try it, read theses questions quickly.

Kinya see two rabbits?

Kinya see the raven in the grass?

Kinya see the hawk in the grass?

Kinya see the hawk on the fence?

Kinya see the gull by the bench?

Exercise 4 Read

Now, you ask these questions using "Kinya."
Say them slowly using the change for practice.

Kinya have dinner with us?

Kinya stay till tomorrow?

Kinya call me later?

Kinya wait a little bit?

Kinya bring me a new one?

Repeat

Now ask to these questions quickly

Kinya have dinner with us?

Kinya stay till tomorrow?

Kinya call me later?

Kinya wait a little bit?

Kinya bring me a new one?

Exercise 5 Present: Can he?   Can she?

Listen to this question.

Can she wash the windows?
Kinshi wash the windows?

"Can she" is changed to "kinshi."

And it's similar with "can he," it changes to "kini."

Kini have dinner with us?

Listen

Kini come over?
Kinshi come over?
Kini stay here?
Kinshi stay here?
Kini have dinner with us?
Kinshi have dinner with us?

Read

Now read these question slowly, then once quickly using the changes you've learned.

Can he come over?

Kini come over?

Can she come over?

Kinshi come over?

Can he stay here?

Kini stay here?

Can she stay here?

Kinshi stay here?

Can he have dinner with us?

Kini have dinner with us?

Can she have dinner with us?

Kinshi have dinner with us?

Exercise 6 Present: Can I?

You can also ask questions using "Can I."

It sounds like "kin I."

Kin I come over?

Kin I call you later?

Read and Repeat

Practice saying "Kin I" a little by reading these questions quickly.

Kin I have dinner with ya?

Kin I stay till tamorrow?

Kin I call ya later?

Kin I wait here?

Kin I getcha somethin?

Finally, you can also use these changes when you ask questions using
What, How, When, Where, Why or What time.

Listen to these questions asked quickly and see if you can hear the change.

Whenkinya come over?

Whatkinya give me for a headache?

Howkin I find the highway?

Wherekin I buy a nice lunch?

What time kinya be here?

Exercise 7 Repeat

Listen to these questions and say them once slowly and once quickly, making the change.

When can you come over?

Whenkinya come over?

What can you give me for a headache?

Whatkinya give me fer a headache?

How can I find the highway?

Howkin I find the highway?

Where can I buy a nice lunch?

Wherekin I buy a nice lunch?

What time can you be here?

What time kinya be here?

Read and Change

Here are some sentences, read them and change them for normal conversation.

I can be home early.

Can you lend me your book?

When can you buy a new one?

Where can I find one?

Can he be here early?

Final Comment

Remember that these are only spoken changes. You should never write them in a paper or school report. Also, remember that you must be able to say the sentence or ask the question slowly and clearly, if needed. If the person doesn't understand the question, "Whatkin I do fer ya?" you must slow down and say it as "What can I do for you?" You must be able to speak using the formal pronunciation, too.

Last, you don't pronounce "kin" when using the negative "can't." I would never say, "I kin't be there." I would always say, "I can't be there." Do not say "kin't."

However, if you ask a question using "Can't" you can say,

Can't ya come over early?

And you can even change it to:

Cantcha come over early?

Cantcha?

Can't you stay a little longer?

Cantcha stay a little longer?

Read and Change

Read these questions using "Cantcha."

Can't you come now?

Can't you have dinner with me?

Can't you keep it a secret?

Can't you give me one?

Can't you stay?

Final Conversation

Okay, listen to this conversation for the changes that you've learned.

Hi. Kinya come over and help me?

Sure, whatkin I do fer ya?

I needta change my oil.

Okay, I'm gunna come over. D'ya have oil?

No. Kinya bring some?

Sure. See ya in a couple a minutes.

Lesson 13 Have you? Could you? Would you?

Introduction

In this lesson, you'll practice asking polite questions. These questions are polite ways of asking about something or asking for something. They use the question forms:

Have you?

Could you?

Would you?

For example, you might ask whether your friend Tom has gone surfing today by saying,

Have you surfed today?

But, when you speak quickly you pronounce it:

Haveya surfed taday?

And you'll see you also make similar changes to questions that start with "could you?"

Listen

Haveya seen the sunset?

Read

Haveya seen the sunset?

Exercise 1 Repeat (reading)

For practice, read these questions slowly changing "Have you" to "Haveya."

Haveya seen the sunset?

Haveya seen the wind taday?

Haveya seen the cat anywhere?

Haveya seen my family on the beach?

Haveya had coffee yet?

Repeat (reading)

Now say these questions quickly.

Haveya seen the sunset?

Haveya seen the wind taday?

Haveya seen the cat anywhere?

Haveya seen my family on the beach?

Haveya had coffee yet?

Exercise 2 Repeat

Now repeat these sentences slowly using "haveya" for practice.

Haveya taken a vacation lately?

Haveya been home yet?

Haveya seen my wallet?

Haveya got a lot a work ta do?

Haveya been sick?

Read and Change

Now read these questions quickly.

Haveya taken a vacation lately?

Haveya been home yet?

Haveya seen my wallet?

Haveya got a lot a work ta do?

Haveya been sick?

Exercise 3 Present: Could you?

You can also use this change when you ask questions using "Could you." It asks a polite question form. For example, listen to this question asked slowly and then quickly.

Could you wait for me?

Couldya wait fer me?

"Could you" can change to "couldya" when spoken quickly.

Listen
Couldya come over now?
Couldya hand me that book?
Couldya drive slower?
Couldya eat with us tonight?
Couldya help me find my wallet?

Read
Now you try it, say theses questions quickly.

Couldya come over now?
Couldya hand me that book?
Couldya drive slower?
Couldya eat with us tonight?
Couldya help me find my wallet?

Exercise 4 Read and Change

Now, you change these questions using "Couldya."
Say them slowly using the change for practice.

Couldya have dinner with us?

Couldya stay longer?

Couldya call me later?

Couldya wait a little bit?

Couldya bring me one?

Present: Could you?

Saying "Couldya" when you ask a question is not the fastest way that I say it.
I often shorten it to say, "Couldja?" "Couldja?"

Now listen to these questions and say them quickly

Couldja have dinner with us?

Couldja stay longer?

Couldja call me later?

Couldja wait a little bit?

Couldja bring me one?

Exercise 5 Present: Would you?

Polite questions beginning with "Would" have the same change as "Could."

Listen to this question.

Would you like to go surfing?
Wouldya like ta go surfing?

'Would you' is changed to "Wouldya'

Wouldya like ta go surfing?

Listen

Would you like to take a walk?
Wouldya like ta take a walk?
Would you like to have coffee?
Wouldya like ta have coffee?
Would you like to see the sunset?
Wouldya like ta see the sunset?

Read

Now read these question once slowly, then once quickly using the changes you've learned.

Would you like to go surfing?

Wouldya like ta go surfing?

Would you like to take a walk?

Wouldya like ta take a walk?

Would you like to have coffee?

Wouldya like ta have coffe?

Would you like to see the sunset?

Wouldya like ta see the sunset?

Would you like to own a cat?

Wouldya like ta own a cat?

Exercise 6 Present: Would you?

You can also shorten "Wouldya" slightly to pronounce it "Wouldja."

Wouldja like ta come over?
Wouldja like ta come over?

Read and Change

Practice saying Wouldja a little by reading this questions quickly.

Would you have dinner with me?
Would you hand me my book?
Would you take me home now?
Would you call a taxi?
Would you hold my coat?

Exercise 7 Present: When would you?

Finally, you can also use these changes when asking questions using How, When, Where, Why or What time.

Listen to these questions asked quickly and see if you can hear the change.

When wouldja come over?

Who wouldja like ta invite?

How wouldja get there?

What time couldja come?

Where wouldja stay?

Repeat

Listen to these questions and say them once slowly and once quickly, making the change.

Have you seen my friend?

Haveya seen my friend?

Could you come over?

Couldya come over?

Would you lend me twenty dollars?

Wouldja lend me twenty dollars?

When could you get here?

When couldja get here?

How would you do that?

How wouldja do that?

Comment

Last, you can also ask polite questions using "Couldn't you" or "Wouldn't you." For example, you might ask if someone can come now by saying,

Couldn't you come now?

Or you might politely ask if someone wants to see the sunset by saying,

Wouldn't you like to see the sunset?

In this case you can ask this quickly using "Couldn'tcha" or "Wouldn'tcha"

Couldn'tcha come now?
Wouldn'tcha like ta see the sunset?

Read and Change

Read these questions using "Couldn'tcha" and "Wouldn'tcha."

Couldn't you come now?
Couldn't you have dinner with me?
Wouldn't you rather stay home?
Wouldn't you need more money?
Why wouldn't you go with her?

Final Conversation

Listen for the changes that you've learned.

Hi. Wouldja like ta see a coupla pictures? Come over.

Here's Claire and Ryan. What wouldja say is their favorite color?

Wouldja say purple?

Haveya noticed her watch?

It's purple.

Wouldja like ta see another picture?

Wouldja take a look at that! Wow!

Lesson 14 Him Her Them

Introduction: Present Him

Next you'll learn some small changes that are very common in conversations. These changes are made with the words

Him
Her
Them

These are small pronunciation changes, but very common. Knowing them will help you understand what is being said quickly to you.

Listen to this sentence for the change to "him."

I gave the book to him.
I gave the book toim.

Instead of saying,
I gave the book to him.

I said,
I gave the book toim.

Here, listen to these sentences for the change.

I gavim the book.

I gavim the book.

The words "him" change to the "im" sound.

Listen

Haveya seenim?

Read

Haveya seenim?

Exercise 1 Repeat (reading)

Listen for the change to "him."

Can you see him drumming?
Kinya seeim drumming?

"See him" changes to "seeim."

Kinya seeim drumming?

For practice, read these sentences slowly changing "him" to "im."

I gavim the book.
I gavim the money.
I gavim the ticket.
I gavim the check.
I gavim the car.

Repeat (reading)
Now repeat these sentences quickly.

I gavim the book.
I gavim the money.
I gavim the ticket.
I gavim the check.
I gavim the car.

Exercise 2 Read and Change

Read and repeat these questions slowly using the change for practice.

Haveya seenim?

Haveya talked toim?

Haveya calledim?

Haveya worked withim?

Haveya met withim?

Repeat (listening)

Now repeat these questions quickly.

Have you seen him?

Have you talked to him?

Have you called him?

Have you worked with him?

Have you met with him?

Exercise 3 Present: Her

Similarly, you can change the word "her" to the sound "er."

Listen to this closely.

I gaver the book.
I gaver the book.

Now listen to this example.

I talked toer yesterday.

I talked toer yesterday.

Listen

I gaver the book.
I gaver the money.
I gaver the ticket.
I gaver the check.
I gaver the car.

Read

Now you try it, read theses sentences quickly.

I gaver the book.
I gaver the money.
I gaver the ticket.
I gaver the check.
I gaver the car.

Exercise 4 Read

Read and repeat these sentences slowly using the change for practice.

Dya seer?

Kinya seer?

Haveya seener?

Don't talk toer.

Kinya finder?

Repeat (listening)

Now repeat these sentences quickly.

Dya seer?

Kinya seer?

Haveya seener?

Don't talk toer.

Kinya finder?

Exercise 5 Present: Them

Do you seeum in front of the wax museum?
Seeum?

When spoken quickly the word "them" changes to the "um" sound.

Listen

Do you seeum in front of the wax museum?
Seeum?

Do you see them by the aquarium?
Doya seeum by the aquarium?

Have you seem them?
Haveya seenum?

Exercise 6 Listen

Here, listen to the pronunciation of the word "them."

Listen

I sawum by the elephant.

I sawum on the bench.

I sawum near the gorilla.

I sawum walkun with coffee.

I sawum walkun ta the car.

Read

Now you try it, read theses sentences quickly.

I sawum by the elephant.

I sawum on the bench.

I sawum near the gorilla.

I sawum walkun with coffee.

I sawum walkun ta the car.

Exercise 7 Repeat (listening)

Read and repeat these sentences slowly using the change for practice.

Haveya seenum?

Haveya talked toum?

Haveya calledum?

Haveya worked withum?

Haveya met withum?

Now repeat these sentences quickly.

Have you seen them?

Have you talked to them?

Have you called them?

Have you worked with them?

Have you met with them?

Listen

Read these sentences and say them once slowly and once quickly, making the changes that you've learned.

Have you seen her?

Haveya seener?

Would you lend him twenty dollars?

Wouldja lendim twenty dollars?

Have you seen them anywhere?
Haveya seenum anywhere?

Are you going to give it to her today?
Areya gunna give it toer taday?

I told him not to do that.
I toldim not ta do that.

Final Conversation

Okay, listen to this conversation for the changes that you've learned.

I saw Claire. Haveya talked toer taday?

No, why?

Oh, she lost her books and she's lookin ferum.

I foundum near the TV. They're here.

Okay, kinya caller and teller?

Okay, no problem.

Lesson 15 Your   His   Her

Introduction

Next you'll learn a number of small changes with the possessive words,

Your

His

Her

These are small pronunciation changes, but you'll need to know them to understand spoken English easily.

Listen to these sentences for the changes.

Where is your car?

Where's yur car? yur car

Is this his coat?

Is this iscoat? Iscoat

She needs her purse.

She needs erpurse. Erpurse.

"Your" changes to the "yur" sound.

"His" becomes "is."

"Her" changes to "er."

Here, listen to this sentence for the change to "your."
Listen

I gavim yur book.
I gavim yur book.

Read

I gavim yur book.

Exercise 1 Repeat (reading)

Read these sentences quickly changing "your" to "yur."

I like yur cat.

I like yur hat.

I like yur shoes.

I like yur iPod.

I like yur drawing.

Repeat (reading)

Now ask these questions quickly.

Where's yur cat.

Where's yur hat.

Where's yur shoes.

Where's yur iPod.

Where's yur drawing.

Exercise 2 Repeat (listening)

Listen to these sentences said quickly, then repeat them slowly and clearly.

Doya have yur wallet?

Is that yur coat?

Areya gunna take yur car?

Ya hafta bring yur friend.

Ya wanna leave yur book here?

Repeat fast (listening)

Now read these sentences and say them quickly using the changes you've learned.

Do you have your wallet?

Is that your coat?

Are you going to take your car?

You have to bring your friend.

Do you want to leave your book here?

Exercise 3 Present: His

When speaking quickly, you can also change the word "his" to "is."

Listen closely.

I gavim isbook.
I gavim isbook.

Now listen to these examples.

Listen

I gavim isiPod.
I gavim isiPad.
I gavim iscamera.
I gavim isglasses.
I gavim ismoney.

Read

Now you try it, read theses questions quickly making the change.

I gavim isiPod.
I gavim isiPad.
I gavim iscamera.
I gavim isglasses.
I gavim ismoney.

Exercise 4 Present: Her

When speaking quickly, you can also shorten the word "her" to "er."

Listen closely.

She's ridun erhorse.
She's ridun erhorse.

Now listen to these examples.

Listen

She's waitun fer erlesson.
She's wearun ersunglasses
She's wearun erboots.
She's gettun on erhorse.
She's ridun erhorse.

Read
Now you try it, read theses sentences quickl.

She's waitun fer erlesson.
She's wearun ersunglasses
She's wearun erboots.
She's gettun on erhorse.
She's ridun erhorse.

Exercise 5 Repeat (listening)

Read and repeat these sentences first slowly and then quickly for practice.

Is that her hat?   Is that erhat?

Are you going to giver your money? Areya gunna giver urmoney?

Have you seen his dog?   Haveya seen isdog?

Have you played on her team?   Haveya played on erteam?

Have you met his wife?   Haveya met iswife?

Repeat (listening)

Now say these sentences quickly making the changes that you've learned.

Is that her hat?

Are you going to give her your money?

Have you seen his dog?

Have you played on her team?

Have you met his wife?

In casual conversation, you must be able to speak slowly and clearly and speak quickly using the changes that you've learned here.

Say these sentences slowly and then quickly.

Does she have her helmet on?

Dshi have erhelmet on?

Which one is his dog?
Which one is isdog?

Where is your horse?
Where's yur horse?
Can you take off your boots?
Kinya take off yur boots?

Could you help her with her hair?
Couldja helper with erhair?

Exercise 6 Present: Your

Here's one last funny change that you might hear. It's a change that's made to commands that end with T, such as "get."

For example, say you want a person to take their feet off the table.

You might give the order:

Get your feet off the table.

However, when speaking quickly, I would change "Get your" to say "Getcher."

Listen

Getcher feet off the table.

"Get your" becomes "getcher."

Listen

Getcher books off the floor.
Getcher shoes off the table.
Getcher money from him.
Getcher work done on time.
Getcher car worked on soon.

Whenever a word ends in T followed by the word "your," you may hear the "cher" sound.

Repeat

Repeat these sentences that begin with "Put your," but speak them quickly and say, "Putcher."

Putcher coat on the bed.
Putcher papers on the desk.
Putcher car in the back.
Putcher things in my room.
Putcher dog outside.

Listen to these examples.

He bought your car.
He boughtcher car.

He threw it at your head.
He threw it atcher head.

He's got your books.
He's gotcher books.

This may be a less common change, but now you'll know it when you hear it.

Comment: Their

Next, let's talk about change to the word "their." I think this is not a common change, not all people say it. However, you might hear "air" instead of "their."

Listen

I gave them their books.
I gavum airbooks.

Did you hear the word "their" shorten to "air?"

Because I don't believe this change is common, we won't practice it here. But you may hear it occasionally.

Final Conversation

Okay, listen to this conversation for the changes that you've learned.

Hi, whatdya wanna do taday?

I don't know, ya gotcher car?

Yeah.

Kin we go listen ta John and isnew band?

Do I knowum?

The band is named after isdog.

Fat Mike? The band's name is Fat Mike?

Yep. John loves it. It was isidea.

Lesson 16 Had to Did you?

Introduction

In this lesson, you'll learn about some changes that I make when talking about the past. You'll learn two common changes for the words "had to," and when I ask questions using, "Did you?"

You'll probably see that a lot of the changes that you've learned so far are similar when talking or asking questions in the past.

Listen

Yesterday a boat hit the beach.
They had ta save the people on the boat.
And they had ta clean up the beach.

Did you notice that I said "had ta?"

They had ta save the people on the boat.
And they had ta clean up the beach.

Now listen again as I say this slightly faster.

They hadda save the people on the boat.
And they hadda clean up the beach.

Did you hear it? When I speak very quickly, instead of saying "had to" I say "hadda."

Listen closely.

They hadda save the people on the boat.
And they hadda clean up the beach.

Next, you'll practice using "had ta" and "hadda."

Exercise 1

Now, listen to these sentences that use "had ta."

Listen

I had ta get some exercise.

I had ta get some gas.

I had ta walk ta the harbor.

I had ta walk the dogs.

I had ta take a small boat.

Now you try it, read these sentences using "had ta."

Read

I had ta get some exercise.

I had ta get some gas.

I had ta walk ta the harbor.

I had ta walk the dogs.

I had ta take a small boat.

Exercise 2

Now, let's practice using "hadda." Say these sentences slowly.

I hadda stop ta see the view.

I hadda stop ta take a picture.

I hadda stop ta read the sign.

I hadda look hard ta see the plane.

I hadda walk carefully on the rocks.

Repeat (reading)

Now read these sentences quickly making the change.

I hadda stop ta see the view.

I hadda stop ta take a picture.

I hadda stop ta read the sign.

I hadda look hard ta see the plane.

I hadda walk carefully on the rocks.

Exercise 3 Repeat (listening)

Now read these sentences quickly and make the changes.

I hadda go inta town.

He hadda get a new car.

She hadda get somethun ta eat.

I hadda get out a there.

They hadda come early.

Repeat (listening)

Now say these sentences quickly making the changes you've learned.

I had to go into town.

He had to get a new car.

She had to get something to eat.

I had to get out of there.

They had to come early.

Exercise 4 Present: Did you?

Well, you're doing great. Now listen to this simple question. I'm going to say it four times. Each time I'm going to say it slightly faster. Listen for the changes I make.

Did you see the gull walking on the beach?
Did ya see the gull walkun on the beach?
Didja see the gull walkun on the beach?
Dja see the gull walkun on the beach?

First, I spoke slowly and clearly as anyone would in a formal situation.

Did you see the gull walking on the beach?

Then I spoke a little quicker, using "ya" and "walkun."

Did ya see the gull walkun on the beach?

The next time I asked it, I made a small change, instead of saying "Did ya," I said "Didja," "Didja."

Didja see the gull walkun on the beach?

And last, in a very informal way, I just shorted the question word to "Dja."

Dja see the gull walkun on the beach?

In the next exercises, you'll make these changes to simple questions that use "Did you."

Listen

Did ya seeum ridun on the beach?
Didja seeum ridun on the beach?
Dja seeum ridun on the beach?

Exercise 5 Repeat (reading)

For practice, read these sentences slowly with the changes.

Did ya see the waves?

Did ya see iscamera?

Did ya see the raven?

Did ya see the sign?

Did ya seeim hit isdog?

Didja see the waves?

Didja see iscamera?

Didja see the raven?

Didja see the sign?

Didja seeim hit isdog?

Dja see the waves?

Dja see iscamera?

Dja see the raven?

Dja see the sign?

Dja seeim hit isdog?

Repeat (reading)

Now to practice these changes, read these quickly.

Did ya hafta buy a new car?
Did ya hafta buy a new book?
Did ya hafta buy a new pen?
Did ya hafta buy a new ticket?
Did ya hafta buy a new watch?

Didja hafta buy a new car?
Didja hafta buy a new book?
Didja hafta buy a new pen?
Didja hafta buy a new ticket?
Didja hafta buy a new watch?

Dja hafta buy a new car?
Dja hafta buy a new book?
Dja hafta buy a new pen?
Dja hafta buy a new ticket?
Dja hafta buy a new watch?

Exercise 6 Repeat (listening)

You must be able to hear and understand these changes in normal conversation.

Listen to and repeat these questions.

Didja see the hawk?

Didja seeum fishing?

Didja seeim catch a wave?

Didja seeum on the beach?

Didja seeum in the fog?

Repeat (listening)

Now repeat these questions quickly using "Dja."

Dja see the hawk?

Dja seeum fishun?

Dja seeim catch a wave?

Dja seeum on the beach?

Dja seeum in the fog?

Exercise 7 Read and Change

Now say these questions quickly using "Didya."

Did you see him come in?

Did you want to see a movie?

Did you want to go home?

Did you have to stay late?

Read and Change

Now, ask these questions using "Didja."

Did you lose something?

Did you want to stay here?

Did you have to get up early?

Did you have a car?

Now read to these sentences quickly, changing "did you" to "dja."

Did you lose something?

Did you want to stay here?

Did you have to get up early?

Did you have a car?

Exercise 8 Present: Did He?   Did She?

Let's look at two more small changes like this. When I ask a question like:

Did he like her?

I often shorten it to sound like this.

Didi liker?

I say, "Didi" "Didi" "Didi liker?"

And when I ask,

Did she like the view?

I often shorten it to sound like this.

Didshi like the view? Didshi, Didshi. Didshi like the view?

Read

Didi liker?
Didshi like the view?

Exercise 9 Read and Change

Let's practice saying "Didi" and "Didshi" a little bit. Repeat these sentences.

Did he have a car?

Did he need money?

Did he say anything?

Did he like the music?

Did she dance well?

Did she go to school?

Did she have a job?

Did she like me?

Final Conversation

Okay, listen to this conversation for the changes that you learned.

Last night I watched an old movie.

It was called Angry Boy.

Tommy was fightun with is friend.

Mrs Peterson said, "Wouldja just stop it!"

Then she hadda leave the class.

Tommy was gunna leave, too.

But then he saw erpurse.

It was kinda open.

So he hadda go close it.

But first he hadda check for money.

Mrs Peterson said, "Didja find somethun?"

Getcher hands off my purse!

Tommy wanted ta run,

But first he hadda giver ermoney back.

She scaredim.

Later he drew this picture of her.

Lesson 17 When did you? When did he? When did she?

Introduction

Let's continue practicing simple questions in the past. In this lesson you'll ask simple questions using

What did you?
When did you?
Why did you?

You learned that instead of saying "Did you" in questions you can use "Didya," "Didja," and "Dja."

Didya see the whale?
Didja see the whale?
Dja see the whale?

You'll practice using this same changes when asking What, When, and Why questions.

Whatdidya see?
Whatdidja see?
Whadja see?

Let's get started.

Exercise 1 Present: What do you?

Listen to these examples of simple questions that use "Did you."

What did you want to buy?
Whatdidya wanna buy?

When did you call me?
Whendidja call me?

Why did you use a telescope?
Whydja use a telescope?

Now listen to the three changes made when asking these questions.

"What did you" changes to

Whatdidya
Whatdidja
Whadja

Whatdidya see?
Whatdidja see?
Whadja see?

"When do you" changes to

Whendidya

Whendidja

Whendja

Whendidya see them?

Whendidja seeum?

Whendja seeum?

 "Why do you" changes to

Whydidya

Whydidja

Whydja

Whydidya stop there?

Whydidja stop there?

Whydja stop there?

Listen

Whatdidya wanna buy?

Whendidja wana buy it?

Whydja wanna buy one?

Read

Whatdidya wanna buy?

Whendidja wana buy it?

Whydja wanna buy one?

179

Exercise 2 Repeat (reading)

Read these questions slowly to practice the changes.

Whatdidya see?

Whatdidja see?

Whadja see?

Whendidya go kayakun?

Whendidja see the turtle?

Whendja go sailun?

Whydidya go upstairs?

Whydidja press that button?

Whydja look in the water?

Now ask these questions quickly.

Whatdidya see?

Whatdidja see?

Whadja see?

Whendidya go kayakun?

Whendidja see the turtle?

Whendja go sailun?

Whydidya go upstairs?

Whydidja press that button?

Whydja look in the water?

Exercise 3 Repeat (reading)

Now for practice read these questions quickly as you would ask them in conversation.

Whatdidya wanna do?
Whatdidya hafta get?
Whendidya wanna buy one?
Whendidya wanna go?
Whydidya need ta leave early?

Whatdidja wanna do?
Whatdidja hafta get?
Whendidja wanna buy one?
Whendidja wanna go?
Whydidja need ta leave early?

Whadja wanna do?
Whadja hafta get?
Whendja wanna buy one?
Whendja wanna go?
Whydja need ta leave early?

Exercise 4   Read and Change (listening)

Now, listen to these questions, then repeat them speaking slowly and clearly without the changes.

Whatdidya hafta do?

Whadja hafta do at work taday?

Whendidya hafta go ta work?

Whendja have lunch?

Whydja use my phone?

Listen and Change (listening)

Now ask these questions quickly as you would in normal conversation.

What did you have to do?

What did you do at work today?

When did you have to go to work?

When did you have lunch?

Why did you use my phone?

Final Conversation

Okay, listen to this conversation for the changes you've learned.

Hi, Whadja do last night?

Nothun much. Didja call?

Yeah. Butcha didn't answer.

Whenja call? I didn't hear it.

About 8:30.

Ah, I went out ta the store.

Okay. Areya comun over later?

Sure. Whendidya want me ta come?

In about an hour. Okay?

Yep.

Lesson 18: What did he? When did She?

Introduction

In this lesson you'll continue asking questions in the past, but this time learning changes to questions like "What did he buy?" and "Where did she go?"

Yesterday a helicopter landed in the field.

Whydidi land there?

Whodidi come to help?

Listen to the question again for the change I made.

Whydidi land there? Whydidi

Whydidi land there?

Listen

Whodidi come to help?

Read

Whodidi come to help?

Exercise 1 Read (slowly)

Now you try it, ask these questions slowly for practice.

Wheredidi find it?

Wheredidi put it?

Wheredidi get it?

Whatdidi buy?

Whydidi get them?

Read and Change

Now, ask these questions quickly.

Wheredidi find it?

Wheredidi put it?

Wheredidi get it?

Whatdidi buy?

Whydidi getum?

Read and Change

Read to these questions quickly, changing them for informal converation.

What did he buy?

What did he want to buy?

What did he do?

What did he have to do?

What did he eat?

Exercise 2 Present: When did he?

In conversations, I ask questions like, "Whatdidi do taday?"

But that's not the fastest way that I say it. I may also ask the question like this.

Whadi do taday?

Instead of saying, "Whatdidi?" I shorten it to "Whadi?"

Whadi?
Whadi do taday?

Listen

Wheredi go?
Whydi go?
Whadi see?
Whendi go joggun?

Repeat (reading)

Read these questions slowly for practice.

What did he buy?

Whadi buy?

What did he get?

Whadi get?

When did he leave?

Whendi leave?

When did he come?

Whendi come?

What did he eat?

Whadi eat?

Exercise 3 Repeat (reading)

Read and repeat these questions quickly as you might ask them in a conversation.

Whadi buy?

Whadi get?

Whendi leave?

Whendi come?

Whadi eat?

Read and Change

Change these questions to speak them quickly as you would in an informal conversation.

When did he go to work?

Why did he have to be there early?

When did he get home from work?

What did he want to do?

When did he leave?

Exercise 4 Present: When did she?

Next, you'll ask the same questions using "she." Listen to this example.

Whendidshi rider her bike?

This is a very small change from the longer formal way of saying "Did she." Listen to the question again for the change I made.

Whatdidshi do at the beach? Whatdidshi
Whatdidshi do at the beach?

Because this is a small change, hardly a change at all, we'll just practice this briefly. You'll learn another change base on it in the next exercise.

Ask these questions quickly for practice.

Whatdidshi buy?
Whatdidshi get?
Whendidshi leave?
Whendidshi come?
Whydidshi call?

Exercise 5 Present: When did she?

In conversations, I ask questions like, "Whendidshe going riding?"

But that's not the fastest way that I say it. I may also ask the question like this:

Whendshi go riding?

Instead of saying, "Whendidshi?" I shorten it to "Whendshi?"

Whendshi go riding?

Listen
Whadshi buy?
Whadshi get?
Whendshi leave?
Whendshi come?
Whydshi call?

Read
Whadshi buy?
Whadshi get?
Whendshi leave?
Whendshi come?
Whydshi call?

Exercise 6 Repeat (reading)

Read these questions quickly for practice.

What did she buy?

Whadshi buy?

What did she get?

Whadshi get?

When did she leave?

Whendshi leave?

When did she come?

Whendshi come?

What did she eat?

Whadshi eat?

Read and Change

Change these questions to speak them quickly as you would in an informal conversation.

When did she go to work?

Why did she have to be there early?

When did she get home from work?

What did she want to do?

When did she leave?

Final Conversation

Listen to this conversation for the changes you've learned.

Didja hear about Tom? He said he had an accident.

No, whadi say?

He was in his car and hit a tree.

Whendi do that? I talked toim yesterday.

Last night. He didn't callya?

No. Didi get hurt?

No, he wasn't hurt.

So, howdi do it? Whatdi say?

Oh, he was talking on his phone.

He spilled his cupa coffee and hit a tree.

Wow. I betcha he doesn't do that again.

Well, he said he learned a lesson.

He's only gunna drink tea when he drives.

Lesson 19 Should have Would have Could have

Introduction

In this lesson, you'll learn to change words "should have," "would have," and "could have" for conversation.

Let's get started.

I wanted a drink.
I got out the milk.
But it was almost empty.
I shoulda bought more milk.

Did you head the change?

I said shoulda.

I shoulda bought more milk.

Here's another example.
Listen
I shoulda brought more money.
Read
I shoulda brought more money.

Exercise 1 Repeat (reading)

For practice, read these sentences slowly out loud.

I shoulda bought chocolates.

I shoulda bought milk.

I shoulda bought flowers.

I shoulda boughter ice cream.

I shoulda brought more money.

Repeat (Reading)

Now say these sentences quickly.

I shoulda bought chocolates.

I shoulda bought milk.

I shoulda bought flowers.

I shoulda boughter ice cream.

I shoulda brought more money.

Exercise 2 Repeat (listening)

Read and repeat these sentences slowly for practice.

I shoulda eaten dinner.

I shoulda taken a vacation.

I shoulda gone home.

I shoulda bought a ticket earlier.

I shoulda visited sooner.

Repeat (listening)

Now read these sentences quickly.

I shoulda eaten dinner.

I shoulda taken a vacation.

I shoulda gone home.

I shoulda bought a ticket earlier.

I shoulda visited sooner.

Exercise 3 Listen and Change

Okay, so you understand the change. Listen to these sentences and see if you can understand them and repeat them slowly.

I shoulda worked harder.

He shoulda come earlier.

She shoulda stayed in bed.

We shoulda bought more food.

They shoulda stayed quiet.

Repeat

Now read these sentences quickly, saying them as you would in a normal conversation.

I shoulda worked harder.

He shoulda come earlier.

She shoulda stayed in bed.

We shoulda bought more food.

They shoulda stayed quiet.

Exercise 4 Present: Would have

We sat on a park bench.

The sun was bright.

I didn't bring my sunglasses.

If I'd know it was so sunny,

I woulda brought my sunglasses.

Did you head the change?

I woulda.

I woulda brought my sunglasses.

I say woulda in informal conversations.

If I wanted to speak slowly and clearly,

I woulda said would have.

Listen

If I'd had bread, I woulda fed the pigeon.

Read

I woulda fed the pigeon.

Exercise 5 Repeat (Reading)

For practice, read these sentences using I woulda.

Which do you want, the pineapple or the bananas?
I woulda taken the bananas.
Which do you want?
I woulda taken the apple.
Which do you want?
I woulda taken the money.
I woulda taken the iPhone.
I woulda taken the iPad.

Now read these sentences quickly making the change.

I woulda taken the bananas.
I woulda taken the apple.
I woulda taken the money.
I woulda taken the iPhone.
I woulda taken the iPad.

Exercise 6 Repeat (listening)

Read and repeat these sentences slowly for practice.

If I'd had time, I woulda eaten dinner.

I woulda taken a vacation.

I woulda gone home.

I woulda bought a ticket earlier.

I woulda visited sooner.

Repeat (listening)

Now repeat these sentences quickly.

If I had time, I woulda eaten dinner.

I woulda taken a vacation.

I woulda gone home.

I woulda bought a ticket earlier.

I woulda visited sooner.

Exercise 7 Repeat

Okay, so you understand the change. Listen to these sentences and see if you can understand them and repeat them slowly.

I wish I woulda worked harder.
I wish he woulda come earlier.
I wish she woulda stayed in bed.
I wish we woulda bought more food.
I wish they woulda stayed quiet.

Repeat

Here are some sentences, read them with the changes for normal conversation.

I wish I woulda worked harder.
I wish he woulda come earlier.
I wish she woulda stayed in bed.
I wish we woulda bought food.
I wish they woulda stayed quiet.

Exercise 8 Present: Could have

Yesterday was a nice morning.

I was gunna take a walk.

But then I remembered that I hadda do my taxes.

I coulda taken a walk,

but I did my taxes instead.

Did you hear how I changed "could have" to "coulda"?

I coulda taken a walk.

Listen

I coulda taken a walk, but I hadda do taxes.

Read

I coulda taken a walk.

Exercise 9 Repeat (reading)

Yesterday I put a chair in front of my car.

And I forgot about it.

Later I got in my car.

I didn't remember the chair.

When I drove off, I heard the chair fall.

I was lucky.

I coulda had an accident.

I coulda run over the chair.

Repeat these sentences slowly for practice.

I coulda had an accident.

I coulda gone surfing.

I coulda played tennis.

I coulda gone skating.

I coulda washed the car.

Repeat (Reading)

Now say these sentences quickly.

I coulda had an accident.

I coulda gone surfing.

I coulda played tennis.

I coulda gone skating.

I coulda washed the car.

Exercise 10 Repeat (listening)

Read and repeat these sentences slowly for practice.

If I'd had more time, I coulda eaten dinner.

I coulda taken a vacation.

I coulda gone home.

I coulda bought a ticket.

I coulda visited longer.

Repeat (listening)

Now read these sentences quickly.

I coulda eaten dinner.

I coulda taken a vacation.

I coulda gone home.

I coulda bought a ticket.

I coulda visited longer.

Final Conversation

Listen to this conversation for the changes you've learned.

Hey, where were ya last night?

Sorry, I stayed home. I shoulda calledja.

We had a few people over. Ya didn't wanna come?

Oh, I woulda come, but I was so tired after work.

You coulda just sat and watched TV with us.

No, I was a zombie. I went ta bed.

Lesson 20 Must have

Introduction

In this lesson you'll learn changes that I make when I say,

Must have

Shouldn't have

Wouldn't have

Couldn't have

Yesterday we went shopping for dolls.

We went into one store that was crowded with

Dolls and people.

There musta been hundreds of dolls to see.

Did you hear it? In this change

"Must have" changed to "musta."

There musta been hundreds of dolls.

Listen

We stayed in the store a long time.
We musta been there an hour.

Read

We musta been there an hour.

Exercise 1 Repeat (reading)

Say these sentences slowly for practice.

It musta been a good song.

It musta been a good band.

There musta been a café nearby.

There musta been 50 hairstyles.

They musta been there for an hour.

Repeat (Reading)

Now repeat these sentences quickly.

It musta been a good song.

It musta been a good band.

There musta been a café nearby.

There musta been 50 hairstyles.

They musta been there for an hour.

Exercise 2 Repeat (listening)

Say these sentences slowly for practice.

I musta left it at work.

I musta left it at home.

I musta left it at school.

I musta left it in my office.

I musta left it in my car.

Repeat (listening)

Now say these sentences again quickly.

I musta left it at work.

I musta left it at home.

I musta left it at school.

I musta left it in my office.

I musta left it in my car.

Exercise 3 Review

Let's look back and review some of the changes you've learned.
Read these sentences. Then say them outloud quickly, making the changes
you've learned for informal conversation.

I wanna go home.

I got a coupla tickets.

I'm gunna have a party.

Do ya wanna walk in the park?

I was gunna leave fer work.

Hes washun the dished.

I hafta find my keys.

Dya wanna run the 10K?

Willya have dinner with me?

Whatya gunna buy?

Whatcha doun?

Whenya goun ta the store?

Whadya hafta buy?

Kinya see the rabbit?

Kini stay here?

Whatkin I do fer ya?

Couldja stay longer?

Haveya seenim?

Kinya caller and teller?

I hadda get some exercise.

Didja hafta buy a new car?

Exercise 4 Present: Shouldn't have Wouldn't have Couldn't have

Here's another change that you should know.

I sometimes say "shouldn't have."

For example,

The peanut butter looked good.
I bought a gallon.
I shouldnna bought so much.

Did you hear it?

I changed "shouldn't have" to "shouldnna."

I shouldnna bought so much.

You can make this change with

wouldn't have
couldn't have
mustn't have

Listen

If I'd had more money,
I wouldnna bought that car.

Sorry, I couldnna come earlier.

I don't have my wallet,
I mustnna brought it.

Here are the sentences when spoken slowly and clearly.

I shouldn't have gone to work.
I wouldn't have bought that car.
I couldn't have come earlier.
I mustn't have brought it.

And here's how they would sound in conversation.

I shouldnna gone ta work.
I wouldnna bought that car.
I couldnna come earlier.
I mustnna brought it.

Exercise 5 Read and Change

Listen to and repeat these sentences.

He shouldnna gone home.

She wouldnna liked it.

I couldnna gone to work.

They mustnna come on time.

We shouldnna come taday.

Repeat (reading)

Read these sentences yourself.

He shouldnna gone home.

She wouldnna liked it.

I couldnna gone to work.

They mustnna come on time.

We shouldnna come taday.

Exercise 6 Read and Change

Last, say these sentences as you would in informal conversation.

He should have stayed
He shouldn't have gone home.

He shoulda stayed
He shouldnna gone home.

The movie was terrible.
She wouldn't have enjoyed it.

The movie was terrible.
She wouldnna enjoyed it.

I was so sick.
I couldn't have gone to work.

I was so sick.
I couldnna gone ta work.

They didn't stop to talk.
They mustn't have seen you.

They didn't stop ta talk.
They mustnna seen you.

I felt terrible.

I shouldn't have come today.

I felt terrible.

I shouldnna come taday.

Final Conversation

Okay, listen to this conversation for the changes that you've learned.

What timeya go ta bed last night?

I musta stay up till 1.

You musta been tired in the morning.

Yeah, I shouldnna watched that movie. It was too long.

Lesson 21 Give me   Let me   Ought to

Introduction

In this lesson you'll learn the changes that I make in conversation when I say:

Give me

Let me

Ought to

Let's get started.

Hello. No, I don't need any insurance.

No, I don't need any insurance.

Gimme a break, I don't need any insurance.

Did you hear it? Give me changed to "gimme."

Gimme a break!

"Gimme a break!" means "Stop. Leave me alone."

Let me changes to "Lemme."

Let me alone!

216

Lemme alone!

And last, "ought to" means "should."

It changes to "oughta."

I ought to call home.
I oughta call home.

Now, listen for these changes.

Listen

Hey, so glad you called.
Gimme a second.
Lemme tellya it's nice ta hear ya.
We oughta talk more.

Read

Hey, so glad you called.
Gimme a second.
Lemme tellya it's nice ta hear ya.
We oughta talk more.

Exercise 1 Repeat (reading)

For practice, say these sentences slowly.

Gimme a minute ta think.

Gimme a second ta think.

Gimme some time ta think

Gimme your book, please?

Gimme a chance ta talk.

Repeat (Reading)

Now say these sentences quickly.

Gimme a minute ta think.

Gimme a second ta think.

Gimme some time ta think

Gimme your book, please?

Gimme a chance ta talk.

Repeat (Reading)

Now say these sentences quickly using "gimme."

Will you give me a chance to think?

He didn't give me his phone number.

If you give me a second, I'll explain.

She wouldn't give me a penny.

He's got to give me more money.

Exercise 2 Present: Let me

As you saw earlier, "let me" can be changed to "lemme" in casual conversation.

Listen to these examples.

Listen

I take my father to a restaurant, and I say,

Lemme pay for the bill.

I spilled her coffee. I said,

Lemme buy ya another one.

I was late and he was angry. I said,

Lemme explain.

Read

Lemme buy ya another one.
Lemme explain.
Lemme pay for the bill.

Exercise 3 Repeat (reading)

For practice, read these sentences slowly.

Lemme think a minute.

Lemme talk toer.

Lemme buy ya a coke.

Lemme drive ya home.

Lemme borrow yur car.

Repeat (reading)

Now say these sentences quickly for practice.

Lemme think a minute.

Lemme talk toer.

Lemme buy ya a coke.

Lemme drive ya home.

Lemme borrow your car.

Repeat (reading)

Now say these sentences quickly using "lemme."

He won't let me talk to her.

He's going to let me stay at his house.

Are you going to let me come over?

She wouldn't let me help her.

Let me tell you, it was difficult.

Exercise 4 Present: Ought to

As you saw, "ought to" changes to "oughta."

And it means the same thing as "should."

I should go home.

I ought to go home.

Listen

Listen for the change in these examples.

I oughta wash the dishes.

I oughta wash the car.

I oughta go jogging.

I oughta walk the dogs.

I oughta go surfing.

Read

Now you try it yourself.

I oughta wash the dishes.

I oughta wash the car.

I oughta go jogging.

I oughta walk the dogs.

I oughta go surfing.

Exercise 5 Repeat (reading)

For practice, read these sentences slowly.

I oughta save more money.

I oughta talk toer more.

I oughta go home.

I oughta caller now.

I oughta eat better.

Repeat (reading)

Now read these sentences quickly for practice.

I oughta save more money.

I oughta talk toer more.

I oughta go home.

I oughta caller now.

I oughta eat better.

Repeat (reading)

Now say these sentences as you would in conversation.

He ought to know better.

She ought to buy a new car.

They ought to be more careful.

You ought to visit me more.

We ought to go to the concert.

Final Conversation

Here's a final conversation, listen for many of the changes that you learned.

I thought we were leavin now.

Gimme a minute. I gotta find my keys.

Yur always losinem, you oughta keepum in your pocket.

Okay, lemme think a second, they shoulda been right here.

There they are on the floor, they musta dropped off the table.

Lesson 22 And Or Because Get Don't

Introduction

In this last lesson, you'll learn some simple changes to common words and phrases. You'll be Introduced to the changes very briefly, so that you have heard and understand them, and then you can practice using them on your own.

You'll learn the changes that I make in conversation when I say:

And

Or

Because

Get

Don't

Let's get started.

The word "and" is reused so frequently that I sometimes shorten it to the sound "un." Listen for the word "un" in this sentence.

I went ta the store un bought a plant.

I went ta the store un bought a plant.

Listen

It was big un green.

Read

It was big un green.

Exercise 1 Repeat (reading)

For practice, read these sentences slowly.

I walked un walked.

I talked un talked.

I danced un danced.

I laughed un laughed.

I ate un ate.

Repeat (reading)

Now say these sentences quickly.

I walked un walked.

I talked un talked.

I danced un danced.

I laughed un laughed.

I ate un ate

Exercise 2 Read and Change

Now read these sentences quickly saying them as you would in a conversation.

Let me go buy some milk and bread.

I want to come and see you.

She laughed and walked away.

I ought to go and talk to her.

Give me a minute and then come back.

Read and Change

Just for some last practice, say these phrases using "un" instead of "and."

Black and blue

Slow and easy

Wet and cold

Hot and humid

Sick and tired

Exercise 3 Present: Or

The word "or" is changed slightly to the sound like "ur."
Listen

Win ur go home.
Win ur go home.

Listen

I didn't have a choice.
It was take it ur leave it.

Did you call ur talk to him?

I sawim at 1 ur 2 o'clock.

Exercise 4 Repeat (reading)

For practice, read these phrases slowly.

Win ur lose.

All ur nothing.

Right ur wrong.

True ur false.

You ur me.

Repeat (reading)

Now read these sentences quickly as you would in conversation.

I didn't know if I ought to laugh or cry.

Keep quiet or lose your job.

I've got to find it or buy a new one.

I should have emailed her or called her.

I ate one or two just to try them.

Exercise 5 Present: Because

I often use the word "because" in conversation.

I didn't go because I was tired.

But when I speak in conversations, I often shorten it just slight to th word "bcuz."

I didn't go bcuz I was tired.

And then in conversations, I often shortened it even more to the single sound "cuz."

I didn't go cuz I was tired.
I didn't go cuz I was tired.

He didn't stay because he was sick
He didn't stay cuz he was sick.

Read

He didn't stay cuz he was sick.

Exercise 6 Repeat (reading)

For practice, read these sentences slowly.

He left cuz he was angry.

He left cuz he was cold.

He left cuz he was tired.

He left cuz he was worried.

He left cuz he was upset.

Repeat (reading)

Now read these sentences quickly.

He left cuz he was angry.

He left cuz he was cold.

He left cuz he was tired.

He left cuz he was worried.

He left cuz he was upset.

Exercise 7 Present: Get

I frequently use the word "get" in conversations.

I didn't get home till 10 o'clock.

But when I say it quickly in conversations, I change it to "git."

Listen

I didn't git home till 10 o'clock.
I didn't git home till 10 o'clock.

Listen

I didn't git tired at all.

Read

I didn't git tired at all.

Exercise 8 Repeat (reading)

For practice, read these questions slowly.

Didja git angry?

Didja git cold?

Didja git tired?

Didja git worried?

Why didja git upset?

Repeat (reading)

Now read these questions quickly.

Didja git angry?

Didja git cold?

Didja git tired?

Didja git worried?

Why didja git upset?

Exercise 9 Present: Don't

In conversations, you often use the word "don't."

I don't get tired.

However, when I say it quickly in conversation, I change it to the sound "don." Listen for the word "get" in this sentence.

I don't git tired.

Listen

I don work on Tuesdays.

Read

I don work on Tuesdays.

Exercise 10 Repeat (reading)

For practice, say these sentences slowly.

I don like coffee.

I don like work.

I don like pop music.

I don like pizza.

I don like winter.

Repeat (reading)

Now say these quickly quickly.

I don like coffee.

I don like work.

I don like pop music.

I don like pizza.

I don like winter.

Exercise 11 Read and Change

Read these sentences making the changes you've learned.

Did you see that wild and crazy guy?

Did you drive or take the bus?

He left because he had to go home.

Did he forget his book?

They don't come to work today.

Comment

Congratulations, you've completed the last lesson of True Spoken English. During this course, you've learned a lot of changes that native-speakers use as they speak in normal conversation. These are changes that I naturally make when I'm having a conversation with friends.

Remember these aren't written changes. Although I have written then here for you to see and to understand, that was just to help you. These changes are typically made in conversation, when I speak with others who speak English well.

There's nothing wrong with making these changes in your conversation. But you must be able to slow down and use the complete and clear forms of saying them when someone doesn't hear or understand you. English speakers, like me, use these two speeds of speech without even noticing them. So practice and listen for these changes on your own.

Final Conversation

Here's a final conversation, listen for many of the changes that you learned.

Listen to these sentences.

Do ya wanna go have dinner?

Sure, but gimme a minute ta rest, okay?

Are ya tired?

Oh yeah, I just gotta sit down.

Whadja do all day?

Inventory. Lemme tellya it was boring.

Putcher feet up un rest. I'll makeya some coffee.

I don want any coffee, thanks. Couldja git me a coke?

I shoulda stayed home. But whataya gunna do? Ya hafta work.

Gotcha. Ya goun inta work tamorrow?

Yeah, I gotta go cuz I gotta finish a coupla things.

www.ingramcontent.com/pod-product-compliance
Lightning Source LLC
Chambersburg PA
CBHW081148090426
42736CB00017B/3229